BROUGHTY FERRY

THROUGH TIME

Brian King

AMBERLEY

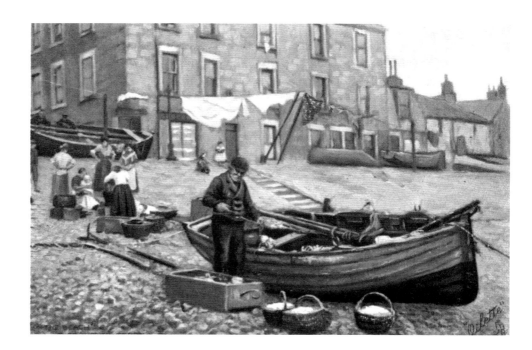

First published 2016

Amberley Publishing
The Hill, Stroud
Gloucestershire, GL5 4EP

www.amberley-books.com

Copyright © Brian King , 2016

The right of Brian King
to be identified as the Author of this work
has been asserted in accordance with the
Copyrights, Designs and Patents Act 1988.

ISBN 978 1 4456 5237 5 (print)
ISBN 978 1 4456 5238 2 (ebook)

British Library Cataloguing in Publication Data.
A catalogue record for this book is available from
the British Library.

Typeset in 9.5pt on 12pt Celeste.
Typesetting by Amberley Publishing.
Printed in the UK.

Introduction

In its history as a populated location, Broughty Ferry has been a fortress, a fishing village, a ferry port, a holiday resort, a commuter town, home to wealthy industrialists, an independent burgh and an affluent suburb of Dundee.

The earliest settlement in the area is thought to date from around 6000 BC but modern Broughty Ferry's origins can be traced to the building of the castle in the late fifteenth century, though it was likely that there was some kind of fortification there prior to this date.

The name Broughty – previously Brochty – is said to derive from the same root as 'broch' meaning a fortress and originally referred to the castle only. The 'Ferry' part of the name has its origins in the boat service that travelled between 'Partan Craig' (crab rock), as the local settlement was known, and what is now Tayport.

A small fishing community nestled in the shadow of the castle, principally in the area around Fisher Street. At the end of the eighteenth century, this area was home to only a few fishermen and their families. Indeed, the entire population of the area at that time was less than 250. The fishing industry grew for most of the nineteenth century before trawlers began to threaten the traditional methods of the Broughty fishermen.

Although fishing was to remain an important element of local life until well into the twentieth century, the seeds of other key elements in the Broughty Ferry story had already been sewn as far back as 1838 with the opening of the Dundee and Arbroath Railway. The coming of the railway, of course, meant that people from Broughty Ferry could travel or commute to nearby Dundee more easily, but the more significant traffic was in the other direction.

As industrialisation began to take hold of Dundee, some sought the fresher air and more spacious accommodation that was only a short train ride way. In the 1840s Broughty Ferry began to expand and the grid of streets between Queen Street and the river began to take shape. The middle years of the nineteenth century saw the wealthiest of Dundee's industrialists seek to escape conditions in the city (sometimes those that their enterprises had caused). Large mansions – the so-called jute palaces – such as Carbet Castle (home of the Grimond family) and Castleroy (home of the Gilroys) began to appear on the hilly land to the north. Broughty Ferry became one of the richest areas in Britain.

The Victorian desire for escape from the overcrowded cities and the perceived health benefits of sea air was not restricted to the wealthy. The less well-off, however, could only make their escape to Broughty Ferry a temporary one. The town became a favoured holiday resort and day-trip destination for those from Dundee and further afield.

By the beginning of the twentieth century, Broughty Ferry's population had grown to around 10,000, and undergoing expansion northward had gathered suburbs on either side in the shape of West Ferry and Barnhill. The town had become a police burgh in 1864 with its own chief magistrate – referred to in later years as the provost.

In 1913 Broughty Ferry became part of Dundee when it was annexed by its larger neighbour. So strong was the opposition to the merger in the burgh though that the matter went as far as the House of Lords before finally being accepted. Any fears that 'the Ferry' would lose its identity in being united to Dundee have proved to be unfounded. More than a century after becoming part of the city, Broughty Ferry is still widely known as a town in its own right, and while officially a suburb of Dundee, it still maintains an air of independence.

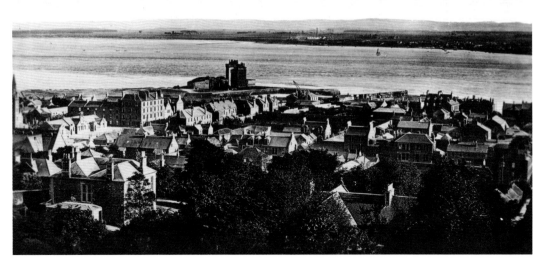

View from Forthill

In the mid-sixteenth century when English troops occupied Broughty Castle, they also built a fort on Balgillo Hill, which consequently became known as Forthill. The modern photograph is taken from a vantage point on Camphill Road which takes its name from the soldiers' encampment in the surrounding fields.

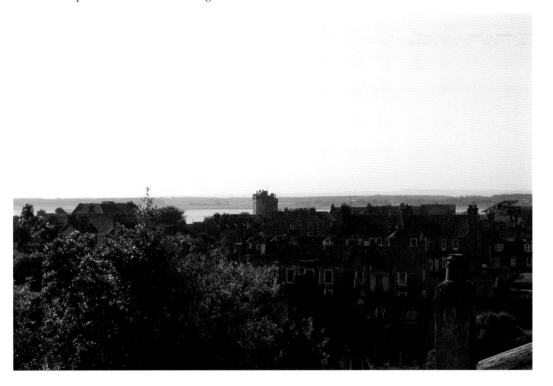

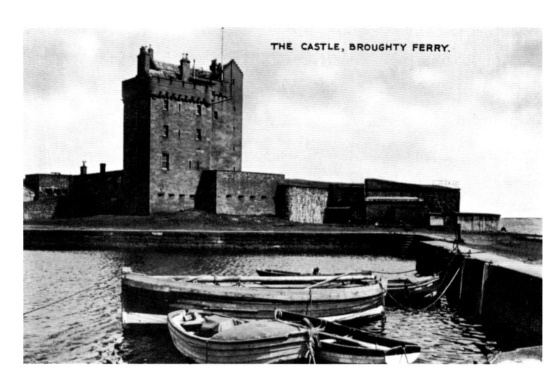

THE CASTLE, BROUGHTY FERRY.

Broughty Castle

Dating from the 1490s, Broughty Castle, which sits at the mouth of the Tay, has enjoyed a varied history. Surrendered to English forces in 1547, it provided a base for their subsequent invasion of Dundee. Recaptured by the Scots with French help in 1550, it was attacked again by General Monck the following year, when Cromwell's army invaded Dundee.

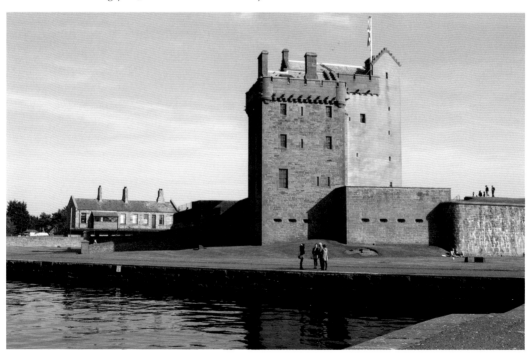

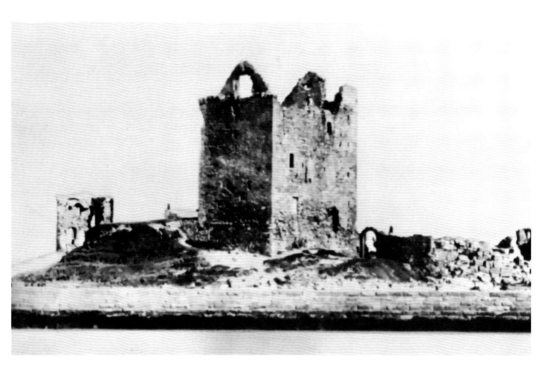

Broughty Castle
The castle lay derelict for centuries. Robert Burns, visiting the area in 1787, described it as a 'finely situated ruin jutting into the Tay'. Its strategic importance for defending the Tay Estuary saw the castle come into the ownership of the War Office and it was finally rebuilt in the 1860s in response to increased fears of war with France. Today it is open to the public and houses a museum.

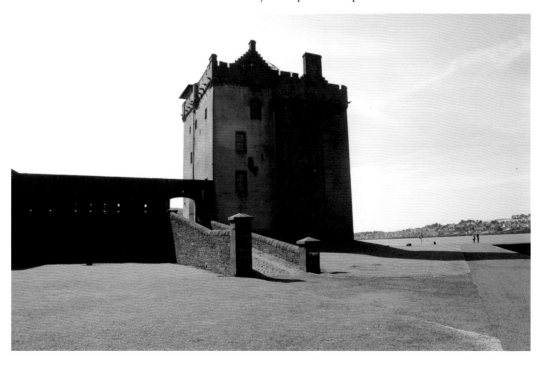

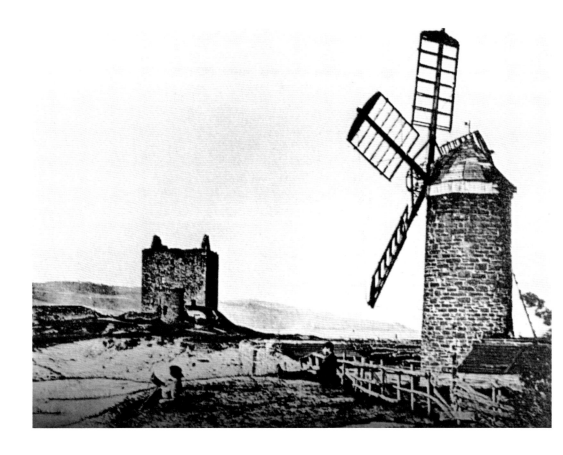

Windmill
This mid-nineteenth-century view shows the windmill that once stood near the castle. The windmill was at this time used by a wood-turner named John Watson to turn his lathe. It has long since been demolished but its existence is commemorated in the name of Windmill Gardens

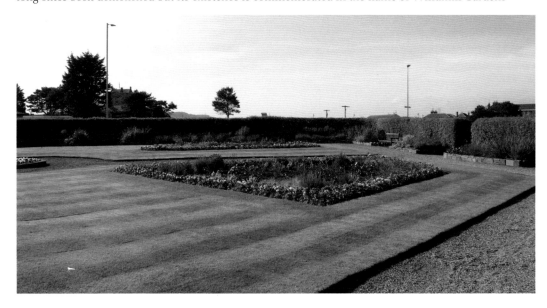

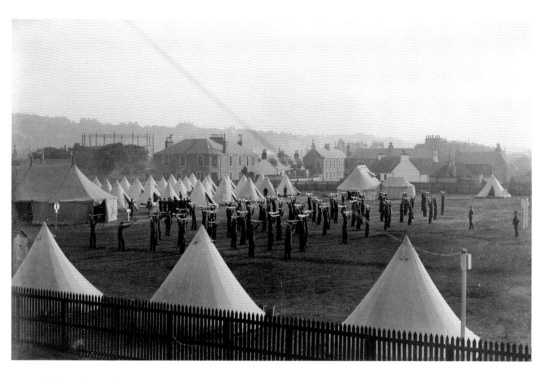

Submarine Miners

The Tay Division of Submarine Miners was set up in 1888 and based at the castle until 1907. They were deployed to counteract a perceived threat to Britain's ports by laying underwater mines. They are shown here at their annual camp on Castle Green, which in more recent years has been home to less militaristic activities such as go-karting and crazy golf.

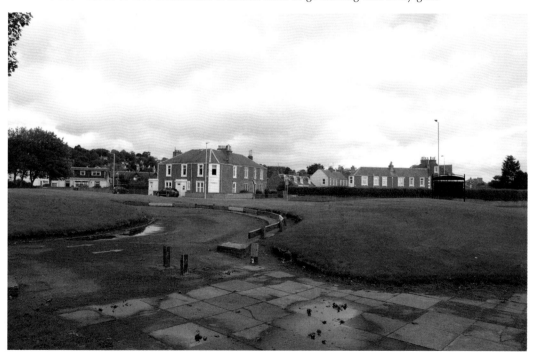

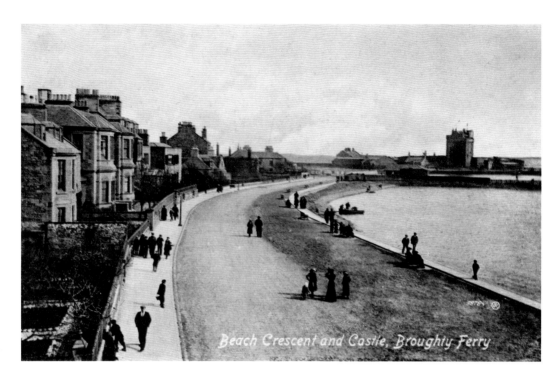

Beach Crescent

Serving to link the castle with the old fishing village, Beach Crescent provides one of Broughty Ferry's most familiar views. It is a view that has not changed much through the years, though at the far end luxury flats now stand in the place of the former Castle Hotel (later the ex-servicemen's club). Beach Crescent retains a strong visible link with the past too in that its lamp posts still bear the arms of the former burgh

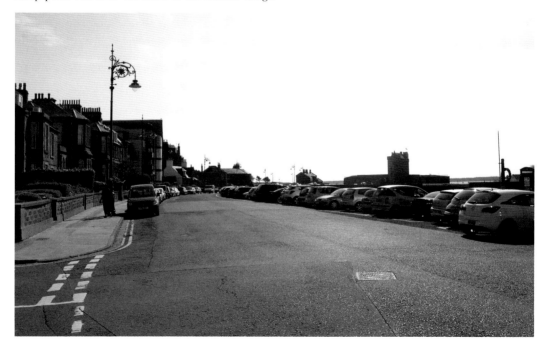

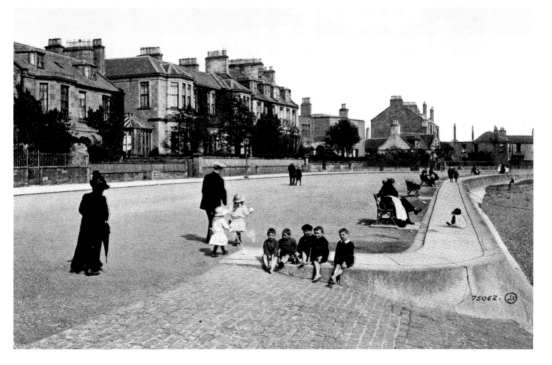

Orchar Gallery

The building at No. 31 Beach Crescent was for many years home to the Orchar Gallery which took its name from James Guthrie Orchar, who was Broughty Ferry's chief magistrate (later provost) from 1886 to 1898. Orchar bequeathed his extensive art collection to the burgh and it was housed here until the early 1980s. The collection was transferred to Dundee's McManus Galleries, though part of it is on display at the castle. The building is now the Orchar Nursing Home

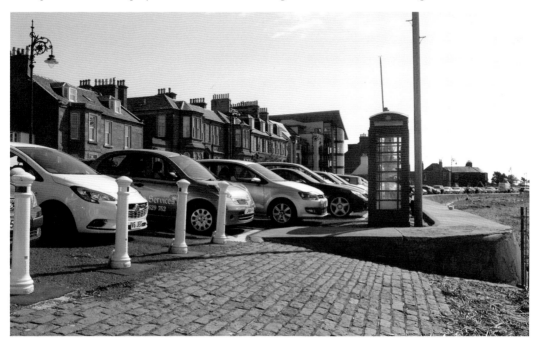

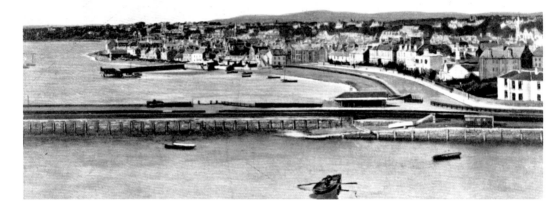

View from the Castle

In the mid-nineteenth century a railway line was built along the pier to connect the Tayport Ferry to the Dundee and Arbroath Railway. It closed when the Tay Bridge opened in 1878 but reopened in the wake of the disaster the following year. The opening of the second Tay Bridge in 1887 saw the line closed once more. The white shed at the left-hand side of the modern picture is home to Ye Amphibious Ancients Bathing Association.

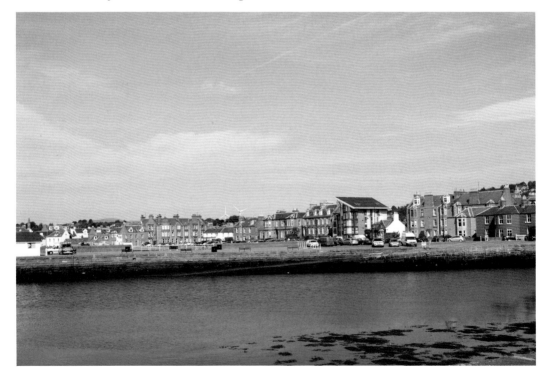

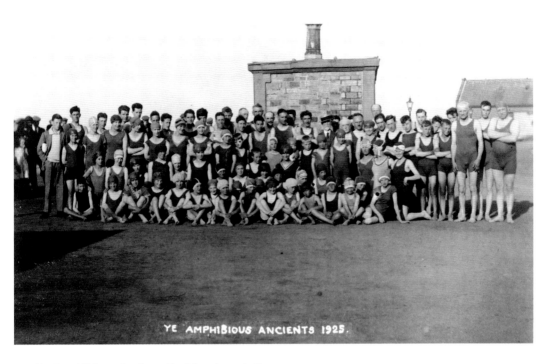

YE AMPHIBIOUS ANCIENTS 1925.

Ye Amphibious Ancients Bathing Association

Ye Amphibious Ancients Bathing Association, known locally as 'The Phibbies', is an open-water swimming association which dates from 1884 when bathers would take a daily 'dook' in Broughty Ferry harbour. The club still organises a variety of events which attract large numbers of participants and spectators. These include the 'Discovery Mile' and the famous 'New Year's Day Dook', which continues to increase in popularity each year.

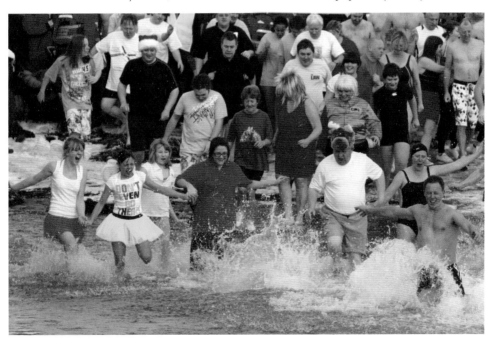

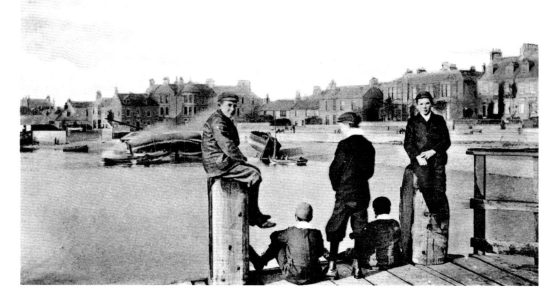

View from the Pier

If these schoolboys were to return to the pier after a century they would undoubtedly recognise the buildings on Beach Crescent, but would be surprised by a notable addition to the skyline. In 2006 wind power returned to the Broughty Ferry area for the first time since the days of the old windmill in the shape of two turbines at Michelin's factory at Baldovie.

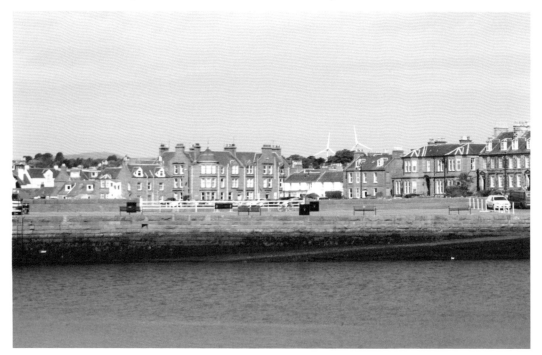

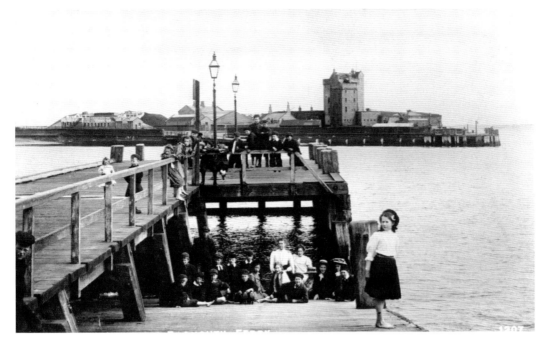

Waiting for the Ferry

The children in the older photograph are probably waiting for the ferry to Tayport. There had been a crossing from Tayport (formerly known as Ferryport-on-Craig) for centuries, but it became regularised in the 1840s under the control of the Edinburgh and Northern Railway. The ferries were initially paddle steamers based at the castle pier, but a motor launch was used in later years.

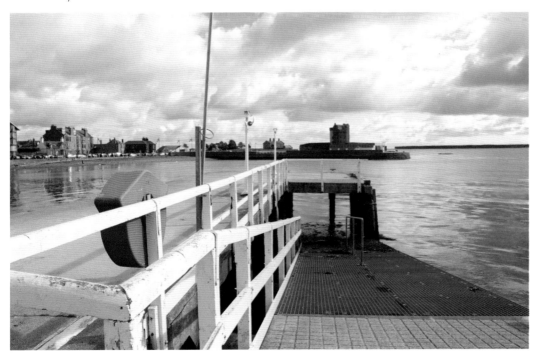

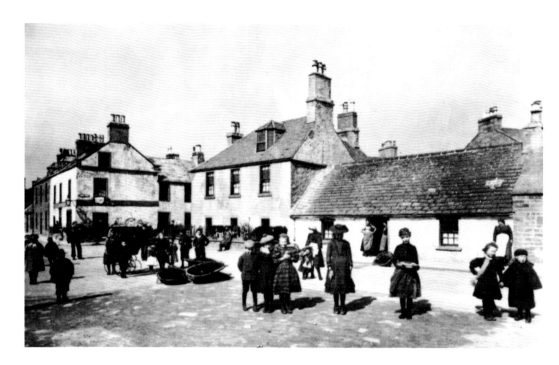

Fisher Street

In the 1880s there were 180 fishermen and more than eighty fishing boats operating out of Broughty Ferry. Increased competition from large trawlers in later years meant that this was the peak of the local industry. By the late 1940s there were only four boats and six men remaining. Nevertheless, Broughty Ferry's origins as a fishing village are preserved today in the name and appearance of Fisher Street.

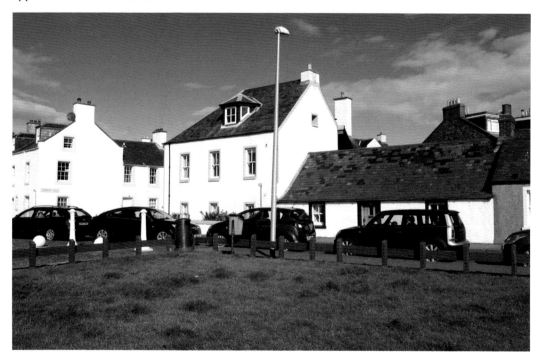

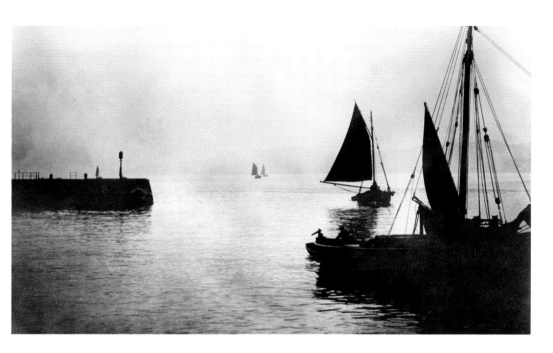

Sailing on the Tay

The sails in this early twentieth-century view belong to local fishing boats. Sails remain a common sight on the Tay at Broughty Ferry, but the type of sailing that takes place today is, thankfully, an altogether more pleasurable activity than that associated with the arduous business of eking out a living from the sea. The modern view looks towards the Grassy Beach at West Ferry where the Royal Tay Yacht Club have taken to the waters since 1885.

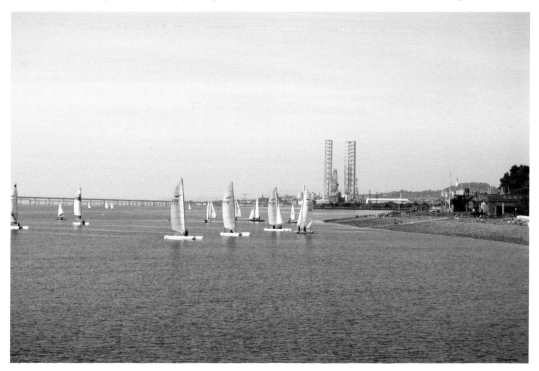

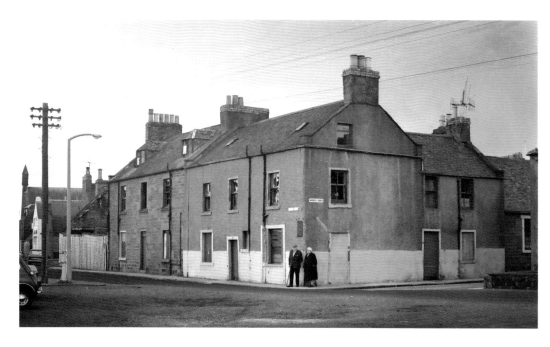

Fisher Street Houses

Looking at Fisher Street today, it is hard to believe that by the 1970s some of the historic properties here had been allowed to fall into disrepair. The National Trust for Scotland helped to regenerate the area through the Little Houses Improvement Scheme whereby the Trust buys neglected 'houses of character' and restores them before selling them on. The benefits to the whole community are well illustrated by these two photographs.

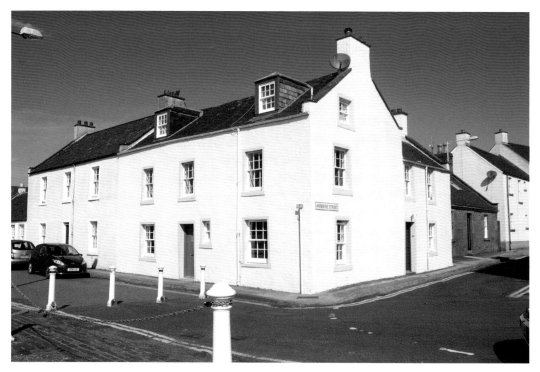

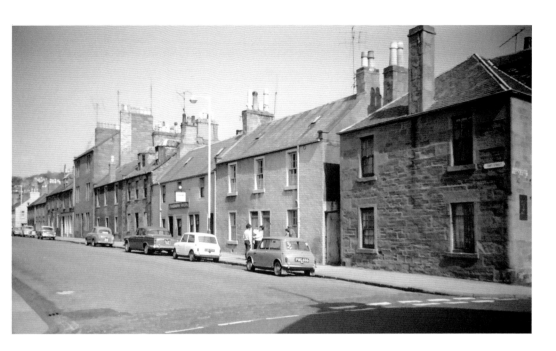

Fort Street

This part of Fort Street was part of the original fishing settlement. The Fisherman's Tavern in the centre of the picture has been in business for almost 200 years. As the modern picture shows, it is much expanded, having taken over neighbouring buildings, and now offers hotel accommodation. In the distance is another historic hostelry whose name betrays its origins – the Eagle Coaching Inn.

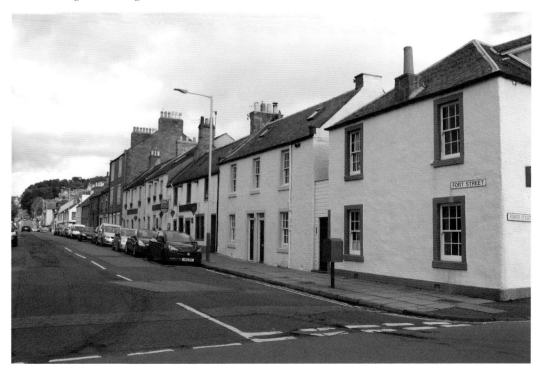

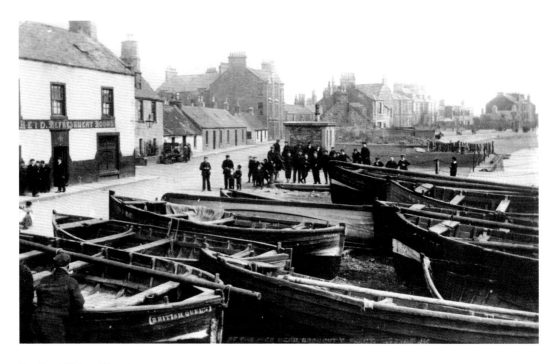

Boats at Fisher Street

Boats hauled up on to the shore were once a familiar site in this area. These days it is a pleasant spot to sit with fine views to the river. The building, at No. 45 Fisher Street, on the left of the old picture was William Reid's Refreshment Rooms, which offered ice-cream among other delicacies. It is listed as a restaurant in local directories from 1888–1907.

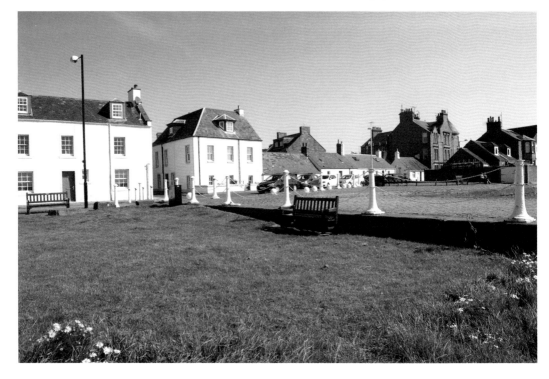

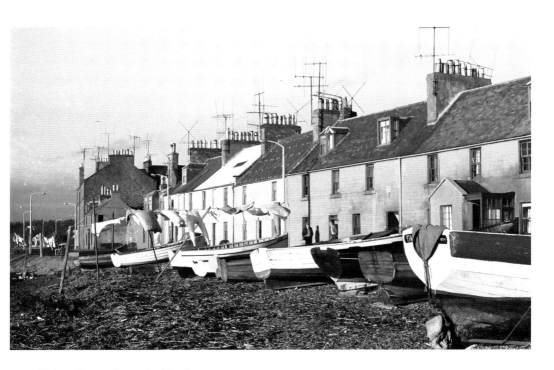

Fisher Street from the Beach

The Fisher Street traditions of hauling up boats and hanging washing along the shore long survived the heyday of the Broughty Ferry fishing industry, as this photograph from around fifty years ago shows. Indeed, both practices continued for many years after this. The modern photograph, however, suggests that they have been consigned to history.

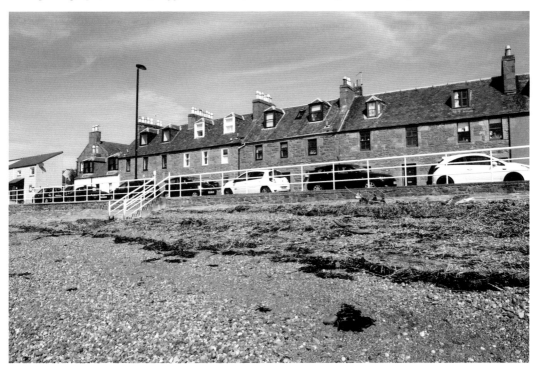

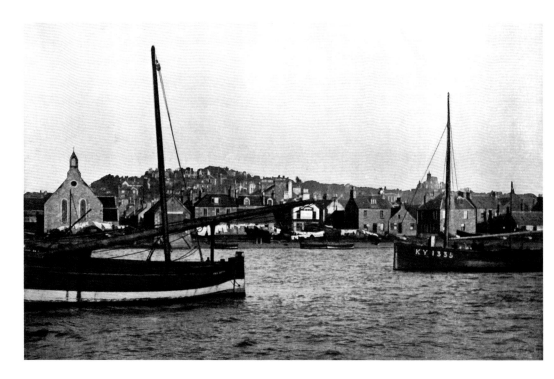

View from the River

This pair of views from the river, captured from different angles and a century or so apart, show the longevity of some Broughty Ferry institutions: the fishermen's church of St James, built in 1889, is still a place of worship today; the lifeboat continues to be stationed at its Broughty Ferry boathouse as it has since the 1860s, and refreshment is still available at the Ship Inn as it has been since 1847.

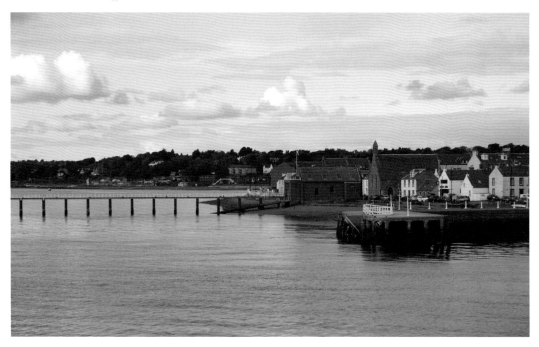

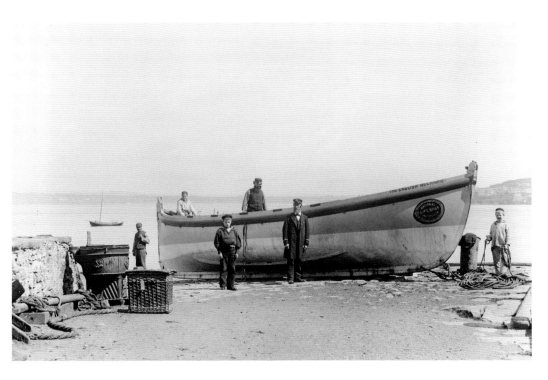

Lifeboat

Taking her name from the magazine whose readers had provided her funding, the lifeboat the *English Mechanic* was launched in 1876 and served until 1888, saving seventeen lives in that time. The current boat *Elizabeth of Glamis* was launched in 2001. For tragic reasons, the most famous of the Broughty lifeboats remains the *Mona* whose crew of eight was lost in December 1959 after going to assist the North Carr lightship

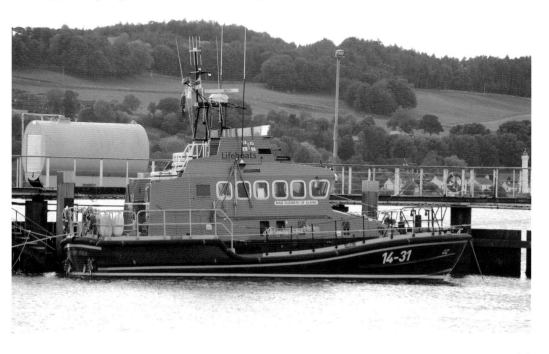

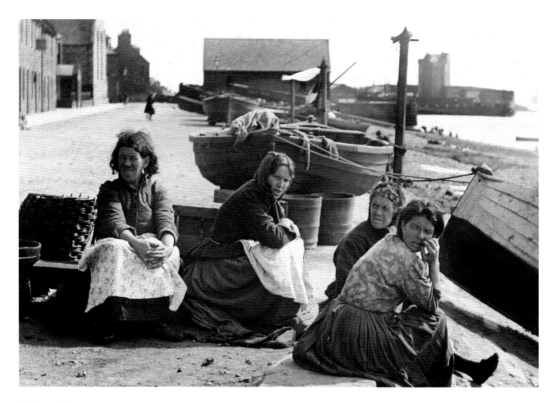

Fisher Life

For Broughty Ferry's fisher folk of the nineteenth and early twentieth centuries, the street and the beach provided a convenient extension to their homes and were used for both work and socialising. The recent photograph shows the divisions between the houses, street and beach more clearly defined, and while the view is recognisably the same, the direct connection with the sea has been lost.

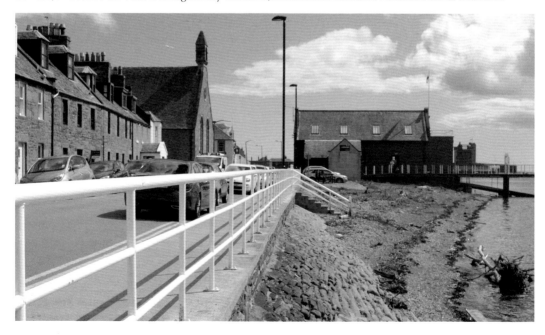

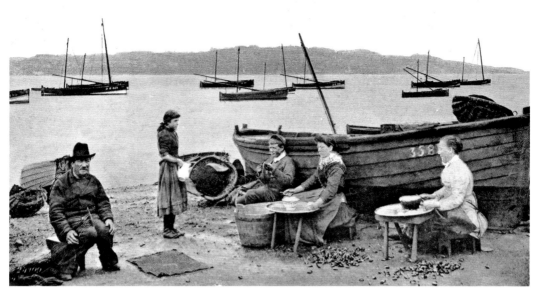

Beach at Fisher Street
All sorts of tasks were undertaken on the beach by Broughty Ferry's fishing community, including the preserving of sails by boiling them with wood bark, the mending of nets, the baiting of lines and, as can be seen here, mussel shelling. Today, the quiet beach at Fisher Street gives little clue that it was once the scene of so much activity.

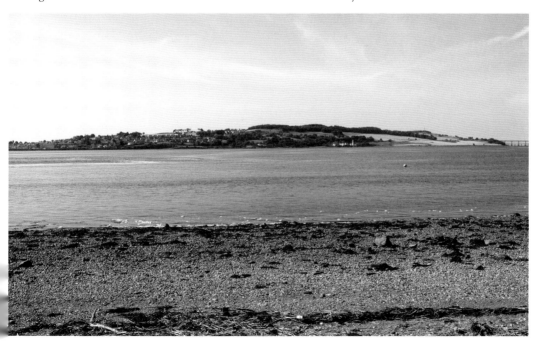

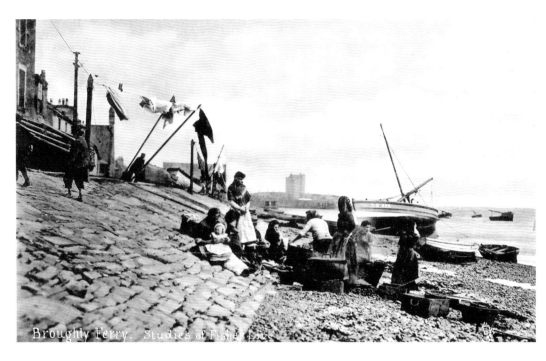

Broughty Ferry. Studies of Fisher Life

Beach at Fisher Street

The fishing community was a close-knit one with strong family bonds formed by intermarriage and shared danger at sea. Women and children were also united by shared work and anxiety about absent loved ones. This view looking eastwards along the beach to the lifeboat station gives a glimpse into a way of life that has now gone.

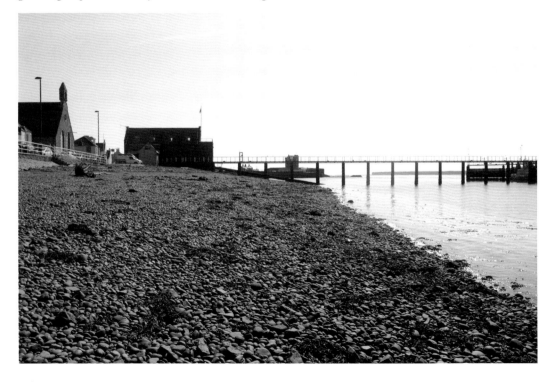

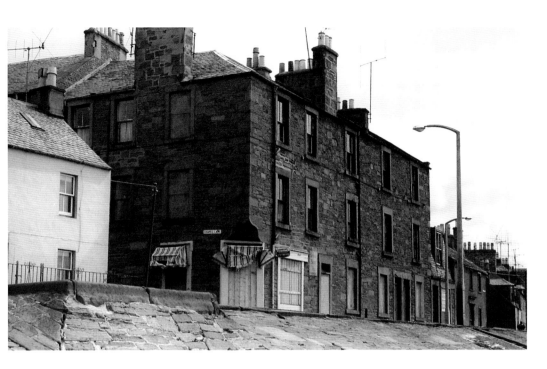

Chapel Lane

The position of Chapel Lane, which takes its name from an old pre-Reformation church that was situated towards Church Street, can be determined thanks to the survival of the house on the left. The tenement building to the right of the picture was part of the property known as Littlejohn's Land and nicknamed Paraffin Land because paraffin was once sold there. This building was demolished and replaced with the houses of Bellrock Square, which date from 1973.

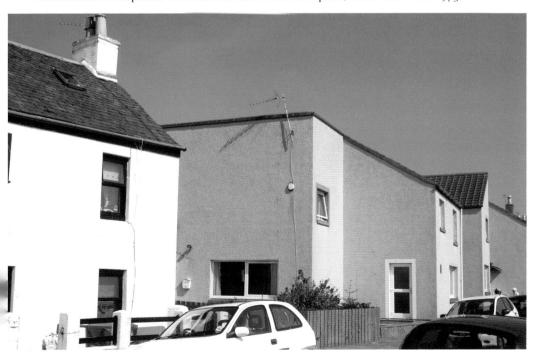

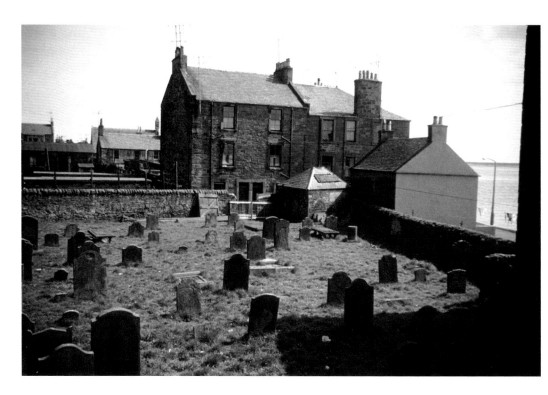

The Old Burial Ground

Long after the old chapel had gone, the burial ground associated with it continued to serve the fishermen and their families as well as the wider Broughty community. It was officially closed in 1867 though unofficial burial continued for a time. In recent years, Broughty Ferry Development Trust oversaw the installation of new gates and information boards that explain the story of this little-known but fascinating aspect of Broughty Ferry history.

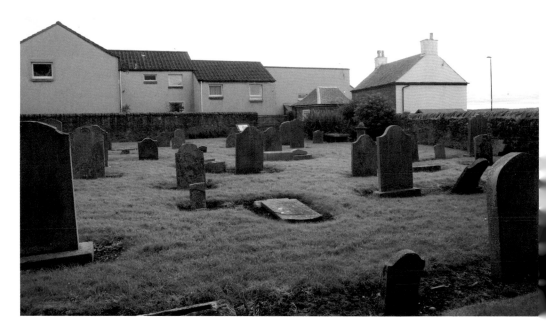

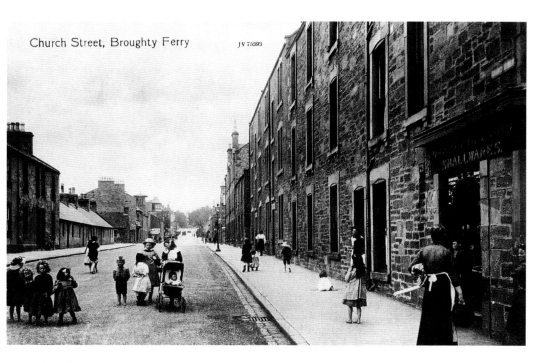

Church Street, Broughty Ferry   JV 75393

Church Street

Along with Fort Street, Church Street serves to connect the old fishing village centered on Fisher Street with the grid of streets that form Charles Hunter of Burnside's new town. The name derives from the same pre-Reformation structure that gave Chapel Lane its name. This chapel was situated towards the present-day Church Street and abandoned around 1670, long before any of the buildings in these photographs existed.

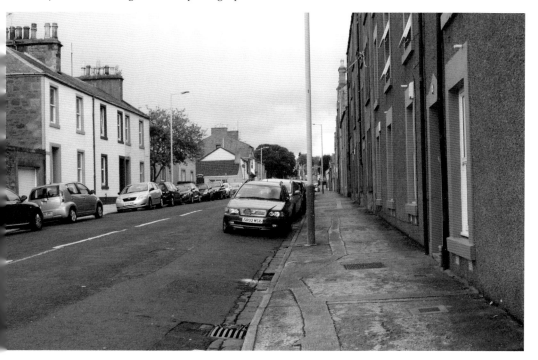

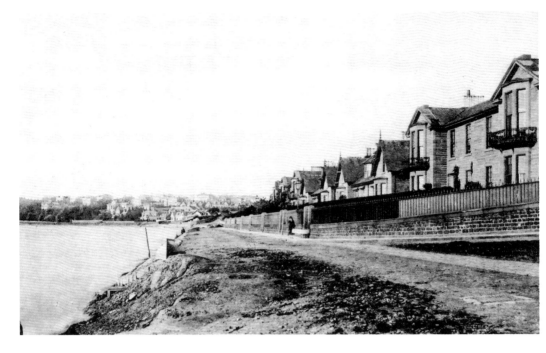

Douglas Terrace

The lands around West Ferry were once owned by the Douglas Home family from which Douglas Terrace derives its name. Appropriately, there is also a Home Street which runs northwards from here. The rough and ready shoreline in this early photograph has been replaced with a neat walkway which extends from West Ferry to Fisher Street

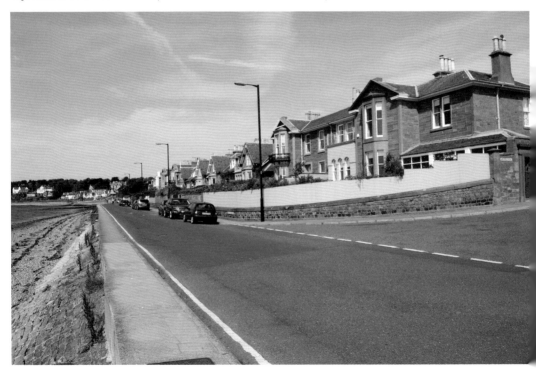

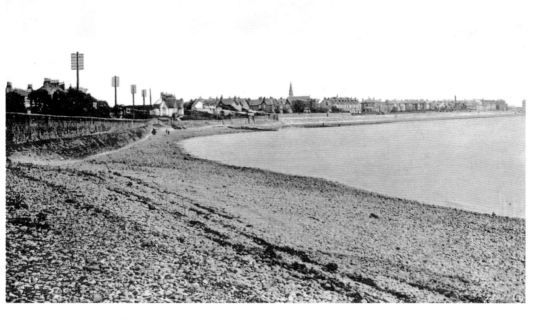

West Ferry Beach

As Broughty Ferry expanded in the nineteenth and twentieth centuries, it gained suburbs of its own in the shape of Barnhill to the east and West Ferry to the west. The view from West Ferry Beach itself has probably changed little since debris from the Tay Bridge disaster washed up there in 1879.

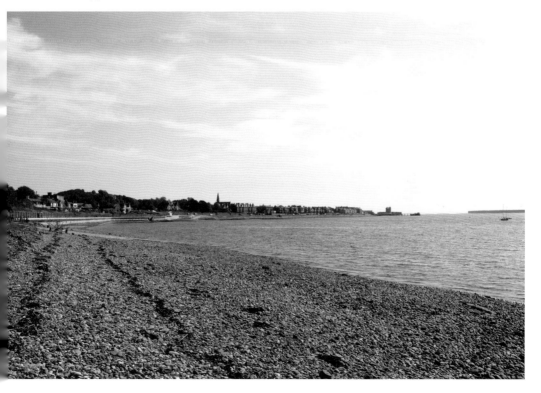

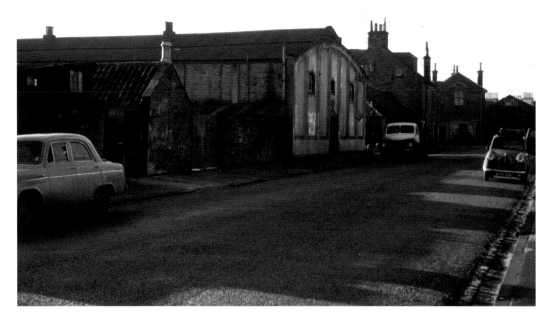

The Grand Theatre, King Street
The rather dilapidated old building in the older photograph opened as The Grand Theatre just over a century ago. In the 1930s it became the New Grand Cinema. In 1962 the site, which was once considered as a possible home for an ice rink, came into the ownership of the local council and is now given over to housing.

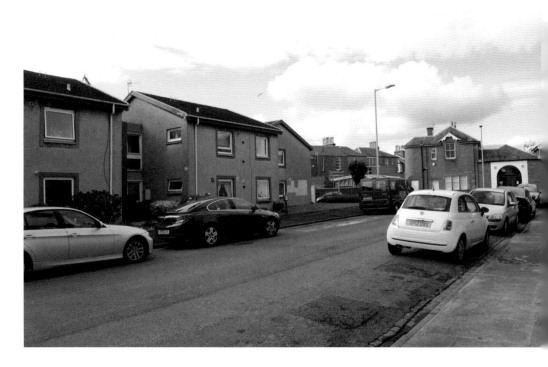

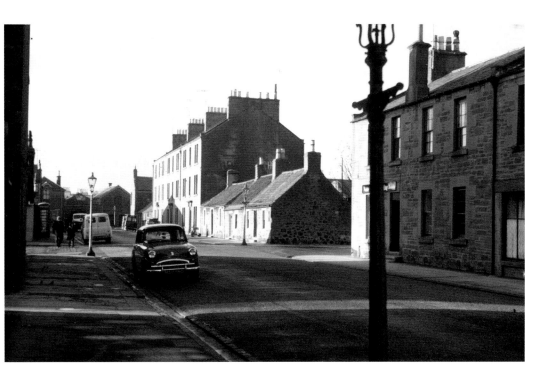

King Street

Unlike its southern counterpart, the northern side of King Street at its junction with Church Street has changed little since this view was captured in the 1960s. The traditional red telephone box on the south side does survive, albeit in a slightly different position

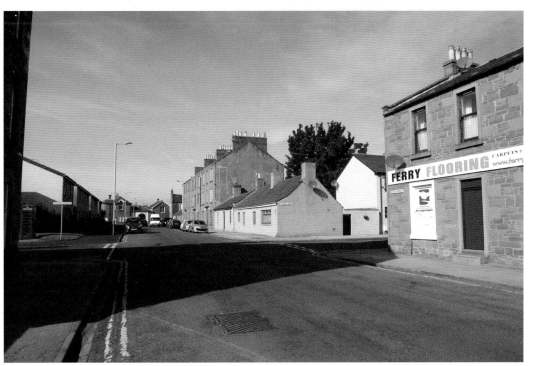

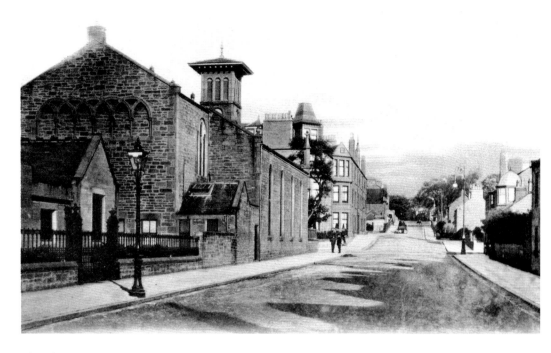

Church Street

There was a church on Church Street in much more recent times than the pre-Reformation chapel that gave the street its name. Broughty Ferry West United Free Church had its origins in the Disruption of 1843 – a major schism in the Church of Scotland. Work began on the church that year and it was completed soon after. The site is now occupied by the Windsor Court flats.

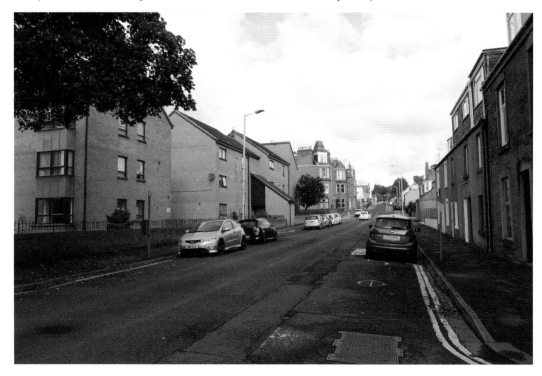

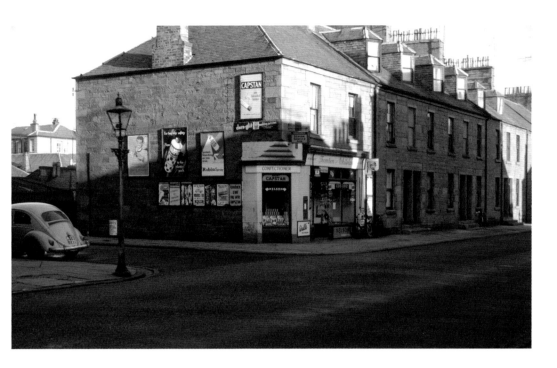

King Street at Lawrence Street

This scene is little changed in the fifty years or so that separate the photographs. The most notable changes are to be found in the style of the advertisements on the wall at Lawrence Street as well the disappearance of the old gas lamp post and the advent of satellite dishes on the King Street flats. The increase in traffic volumes apparent here has no doubt led to the introduction of the 'No Entry' signs and double yellow lines.

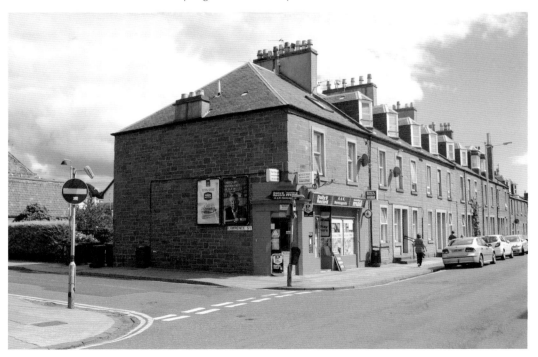

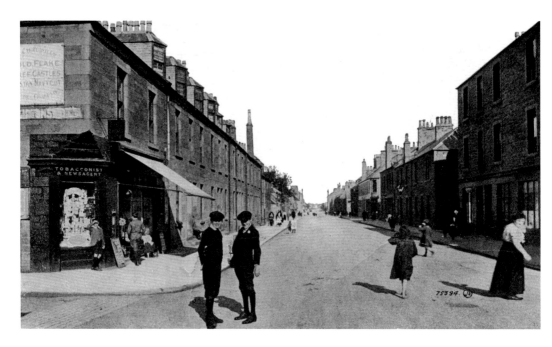

King Street

A wider view from the same corner shows more dramatic change as the old tenements on the right of the picture have been replaced with modern housing. Some things remain constant though, and the postbox in the newsagent's wall still bears the royal cypher of King Edward VII as it would have done at the time the earlier photograph was taken in 1913. However, the name King Street itself commemorates an earlier monarch – King George III.

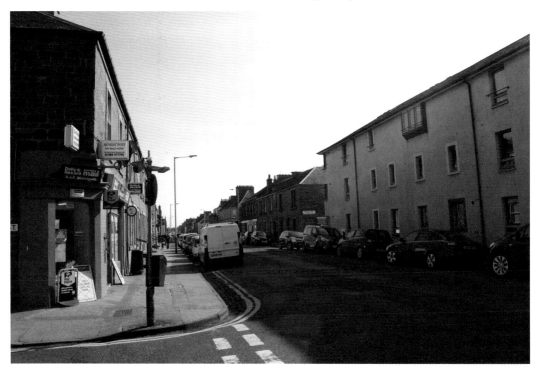

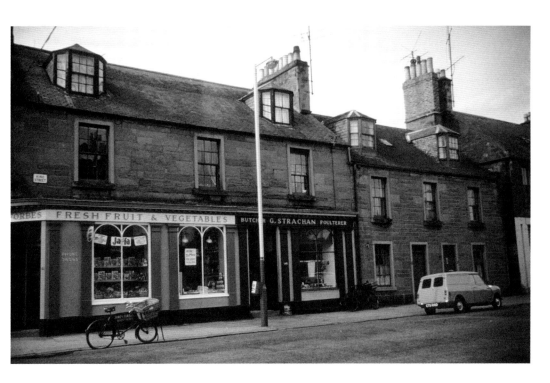

King Street at Fort Street

The changing face of shopping over the last half-century is neatly demonstrated in these two images. In the 1960s view, Forbes's fruit and vegetable shop and Strachan the butcher have their delivery bicycles parked outside while the boutique which occupies the premises today organises its home deliveries through the World Wide Web.

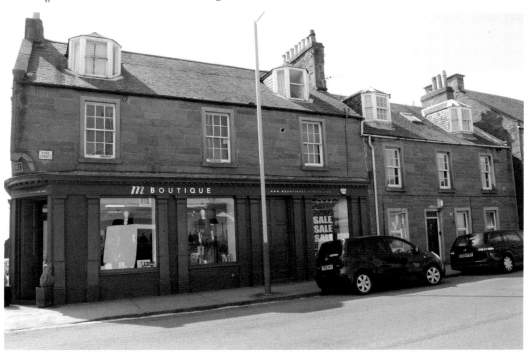

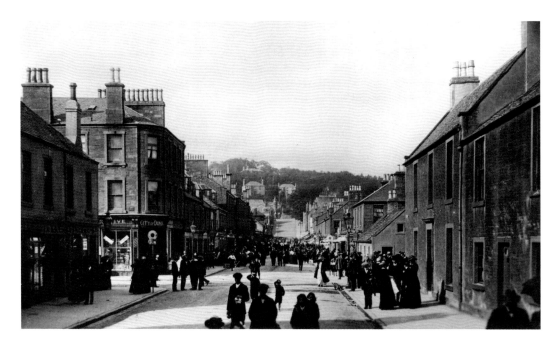

Gray Street

Many postcards were produced of Gray Street, reflecting its position as one of Broughty Ferry's main streets. Most however tended to concentrate on a particular part of the street. This one, dating from around 1913, shows all three sections of the street and demonstrates its prominent place in the grid of streets designed by Charles Hunter of Burnside in the 1840s as it crosses King Street, Brook Street and Queen Street.

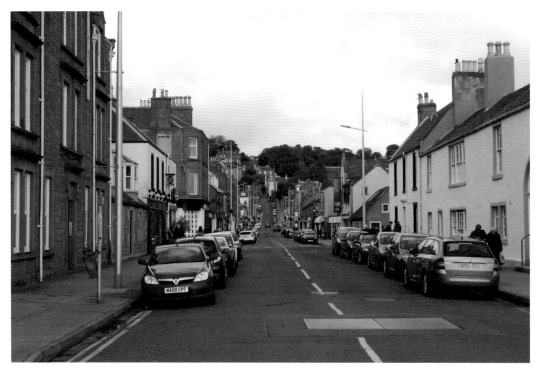

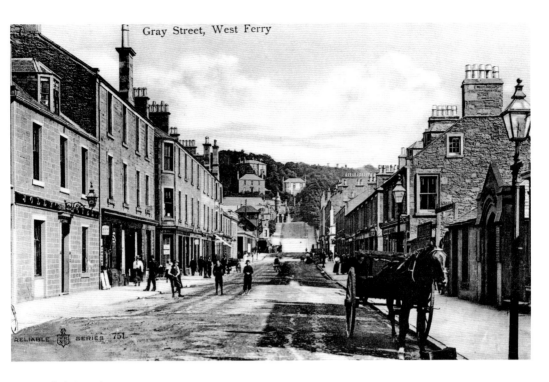

Jolly's Hotel

A little further up Gray Street, this view prominently features Jolly's Hotel, which takes its name from John Jolly who was its proprietor in the 1850s and `60s. In April 2014 a renovated version of Jolly's, much expanded from the original building, was opened by JD Wetherspoon.

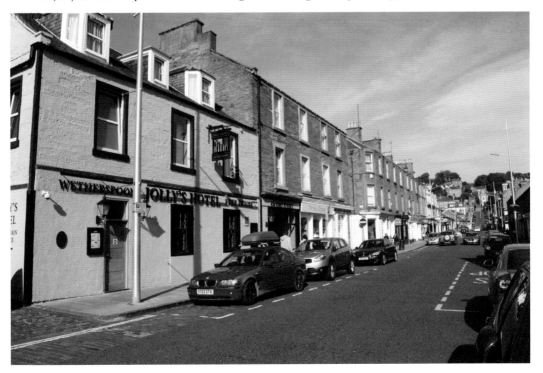

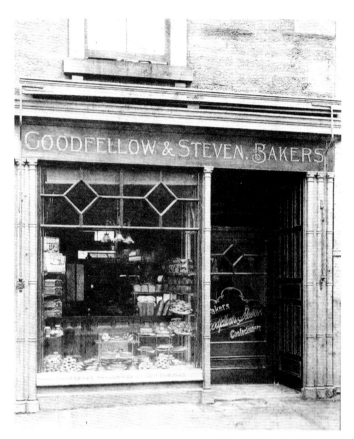

Goodfellow and Steven, No. 75 Gray Street
The well-known Broughty Ferry bakery firm of Goodfellow and Steven was founded in 1897 by David Goodfellow and Margaret Steven. The couple went on to marry in 1900. Their original bakery premises was in Brook Street, but the retail side of the business was conducted from a shop at No. 75 Gray Street. This shop now forms part of a larger premises, but the decorative columns and window design survive, making it readily identifiable.

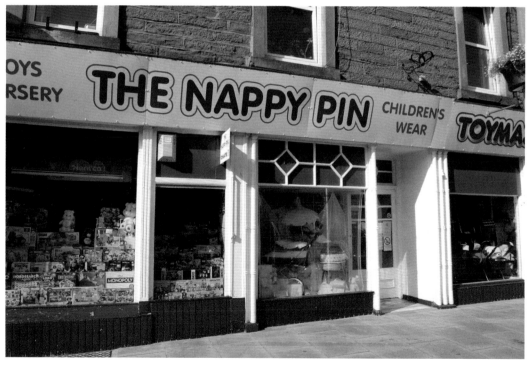

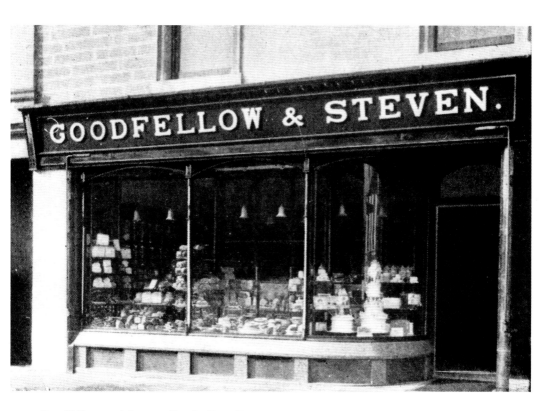

Goodfellow and Steven, No. 83 Gray Street
In 1909 Goodfellow and Steven moved to new premises further up Gray Street and despite opening a number of successful branches elsewhere have always remained firmly rooted in Broughty Ferry.

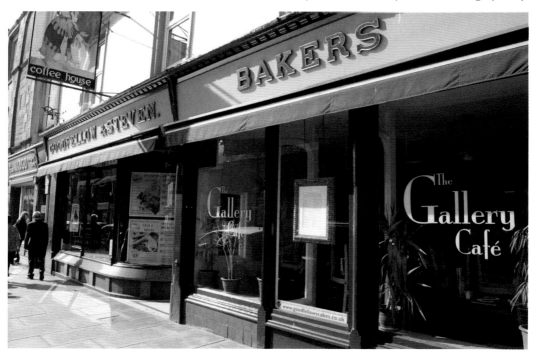

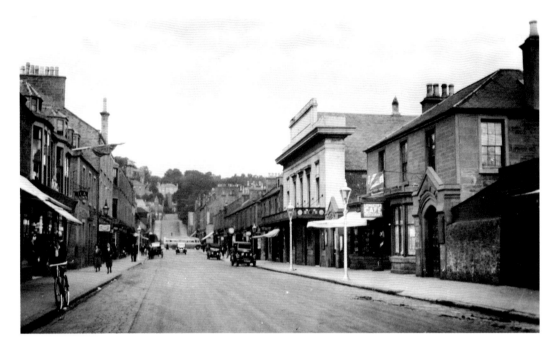

Broughty Ferry Picture House

The Broughty Ferry Picture House at No. 44 Gray Street opened in 1916 and was a feature of life in the suburb until 1963, by which time it had changed its name to the Reres Cinema. The building survives today but has been divided into smaller units. Livingston's Café at No. 40 was bought in 1955 by members of the Visocchi family and another Broughty Ferry institution was born.

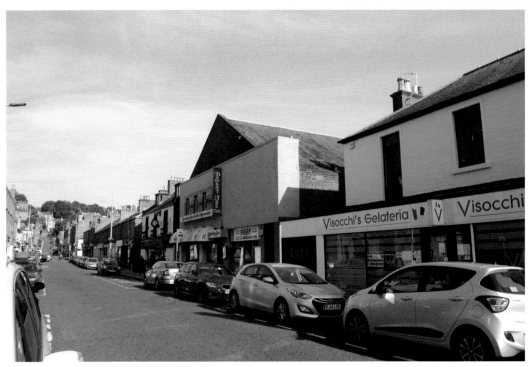

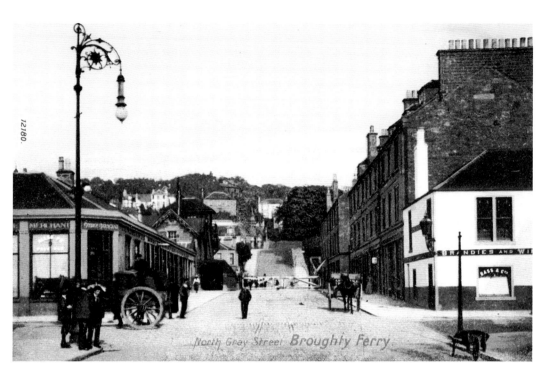

Gray Street

Some aspects of the view of the northern section of Gray Street shown in this old postcard remain noticeably unchanged. The Royal Arch pub on the right-hand side, which takes its name from the arch built in Dundee to commemorate the visit of Queen Victoria, has occupied this site since 1869, and the level crossing still divides this section of the street as it did a century and more ago.

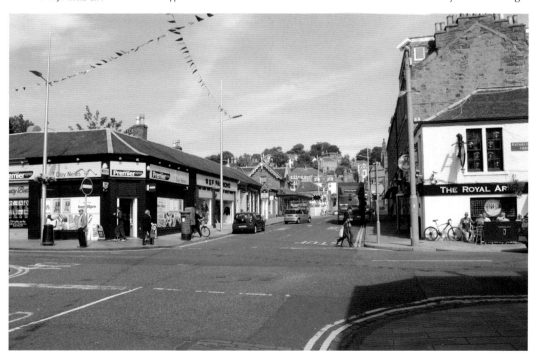

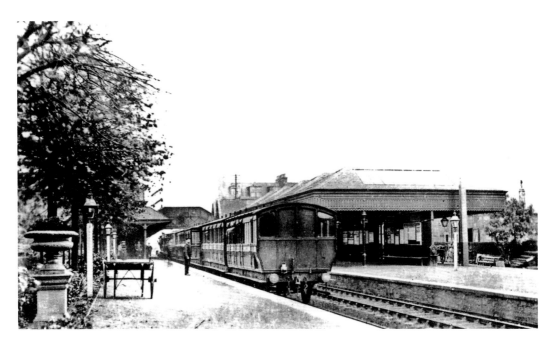

Broughty Ferry Railway Station

The Dundee & Arbroath Railway opened in 1838 and helped to transform Broughty Ferry by making commuting to Dundee affordable for some and encouraging others to visit on holiday. While it has undergone many changes over the years, the station is still in use today – albeit limited – unlike its one-time neighbours at West Ferry and Barnhill.

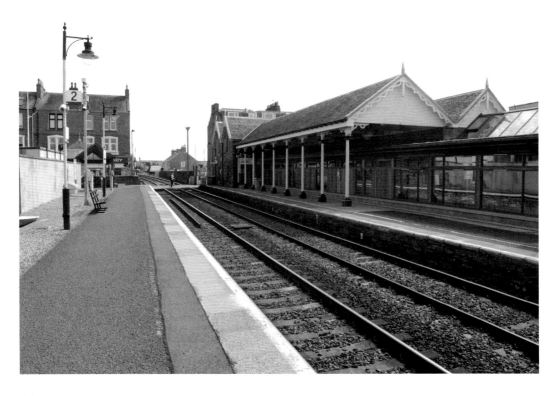

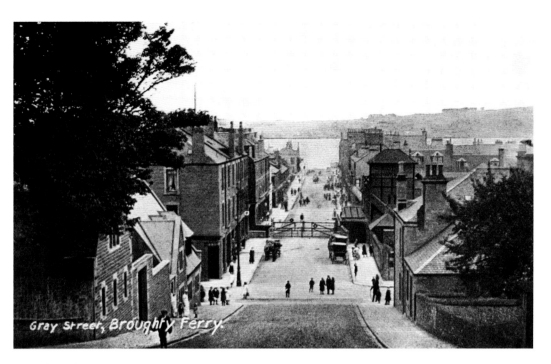

Gray Street

In many ways Gray Street encompasses the whole story of Broughty Ferry. Named after Lord Gray who oversaw the construction of the castle in 1490, it begins (or ends) at the river where the fishing community settled, becomes part of the grid of streets that form the new town of the 1840s and crosses the railway that transformed the town, before climbing the hill towards some of the houses that gained Broughty Ferry the reputation as Britain's wealthiest suburb.

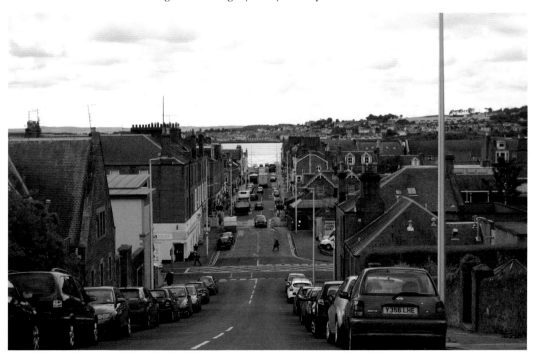

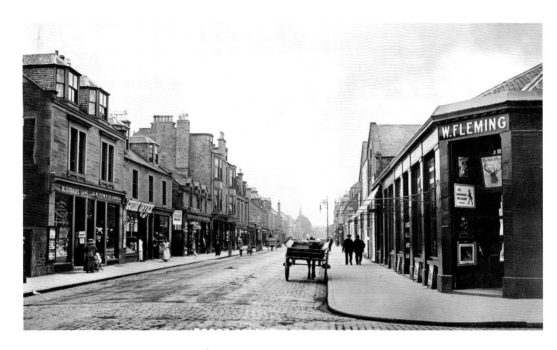

Brook Street Looking West

Just as it was a century ago, Brook Street remains Broughty Ferry's main shopping street. This does not mean, however, that there have been no changes in that period. While all the buildings on the south side of the street in this pre-First World War postcard appear to have survived, those immediately beyond the corner building on the north side have all been replaced over the years.

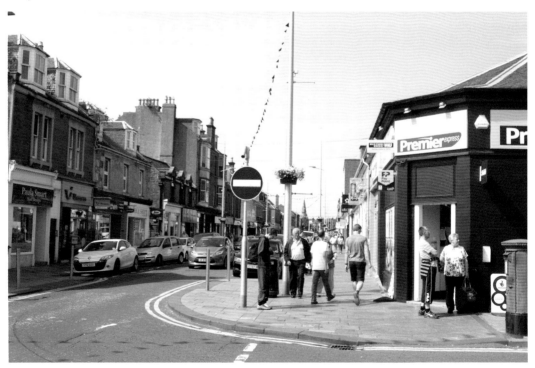

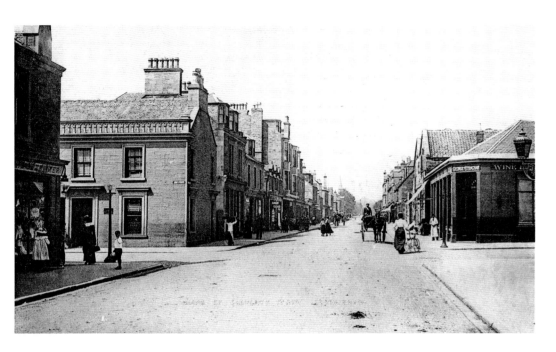

Brook Street

The corner shop at No. 275 Brook Street has served many purposes. In this early twentieth century picture it houses George Strachan's grocers and wine merchants. Later, Fleming and Anderson (see opposite page) had a similar business. Many will remember more recent occupants such as Dorothy's the drapers. In contrast, No. 89 Gray Street has been home to the Clydesdale (formerly North of Scotland) Bank for more than a century, though the building itself was altered around 1912.

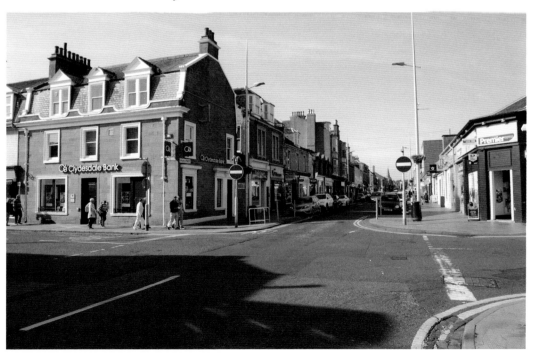

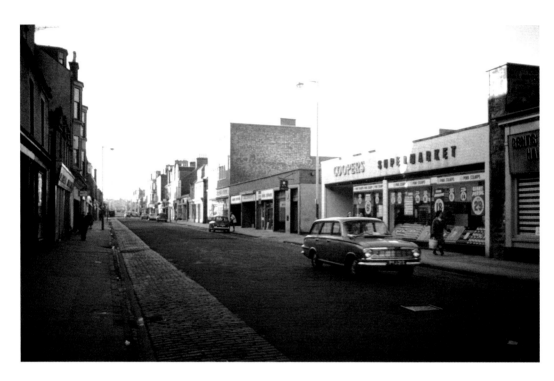

Brook Street

The pre-decimal prices in the window of Cooper's supermarket at No. 261 Brook Street indicate that this photograph was taken sometime prior to 1971 and the quiet streets suggest a Sunday or early morning. By 2015, the supermarket has been split into two shop units and John Kocher's barber shop just visible on the right of the picture is now home to a clothes repair shop.

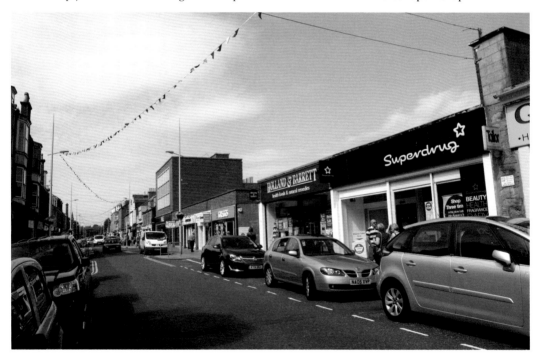

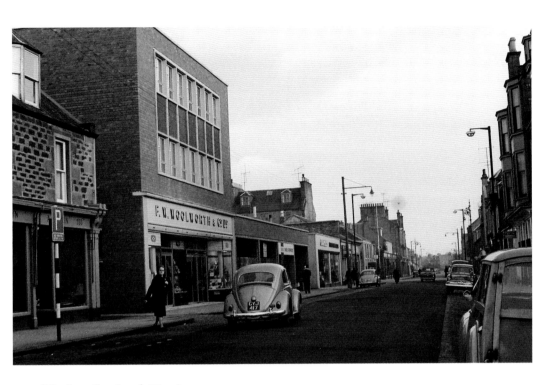

Woolworths, Brook Street

This view of Brook Street is dominated by the Woolworths store at number No. 251 which survived until the collapse of the group in 2008. At the time this photograph was taken even a large shop such as Woolworths would have been closed all day Sunday and for a half-day each Wednesday. In contrast, the branch of M & Co. which now occupies the site is open seven days a week.

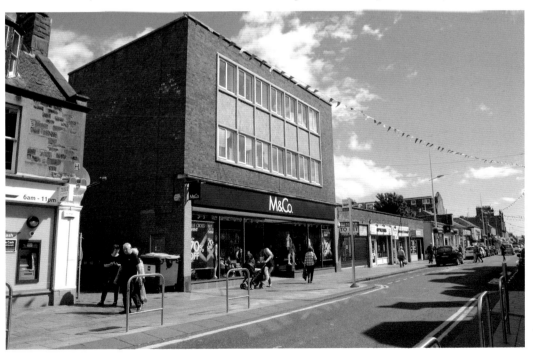

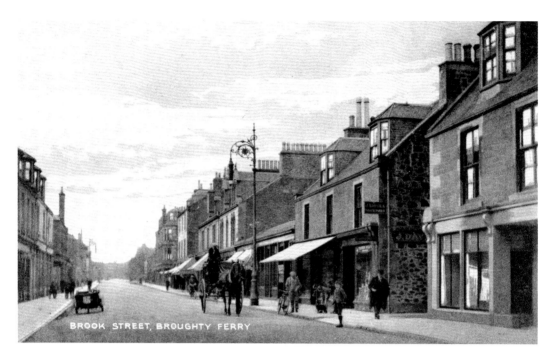

BROOK STREET, BROUGHTY FERRY

Brook Street

Like its counterpart in Dundee, Brook Street takes its name from an old burn which was long since piped underground, even by the time of the earlier photograph here. All the buildings survive except for the block on the right-hand side which made way for the Woolworths building.

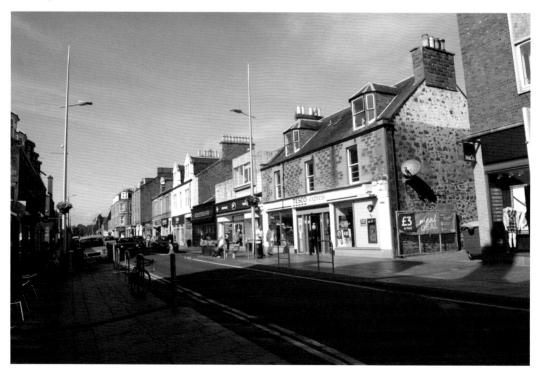

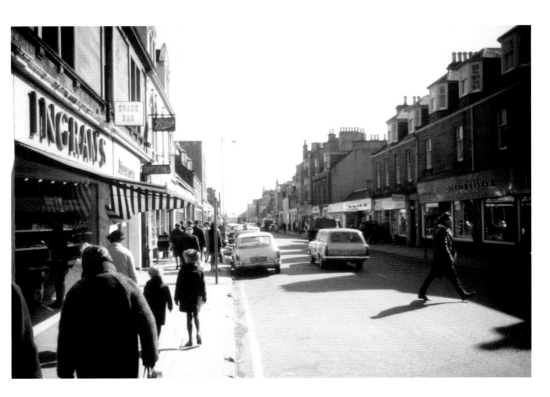

Brook Street
In contrast to the fate of many high streets in recent years, Brook Street continues to thrive, though it is not immune to the wider trends. Branches of larger chains and independent local businesses now sit side by side with charity shops as the recent photograph shows.

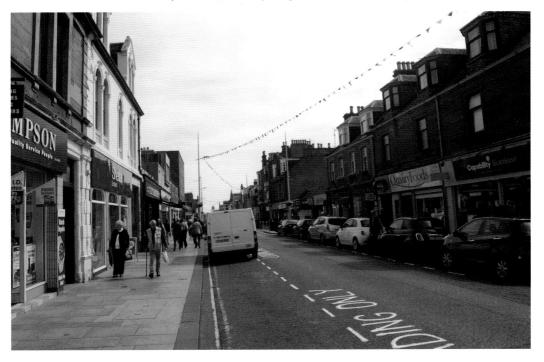

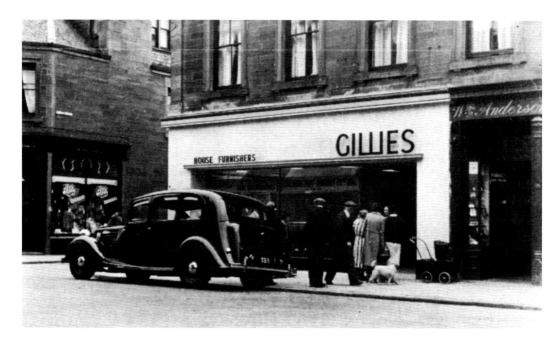

Gillies of Broughty Ferry

James Gillies began in business as a partner in an upholstery firm Chapman & Gillies, based in Dundee. In 1906 Gillies set up in business on his own as a cabinetmaker and upholsterer at No. 206 Brook Street, later moving to Nos 186–188 and finally in 1939 to No. 180. The firm today remains an independent family-run business, still strongly associated with Broughty Ferry, specialising in home furnishing and floor coverings.

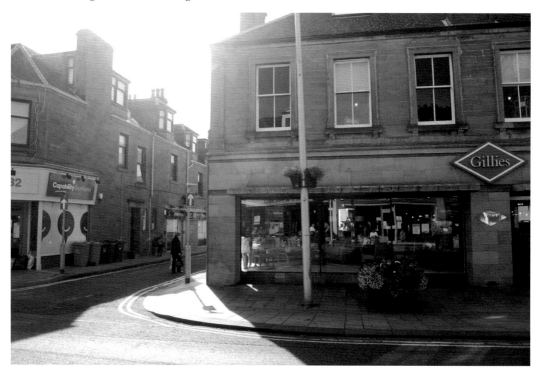

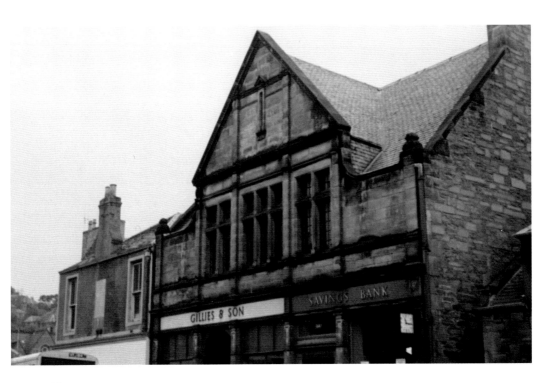

Gillies at Fort Street

Over the years the Gillies business in Broughty Ferry expanded, taking over various properties in Brook Street, Union Street and, as shown here, Fort Street. A new building was added to the Fort Street side of the premises in more recent years, which reflects the style of the existing premises.

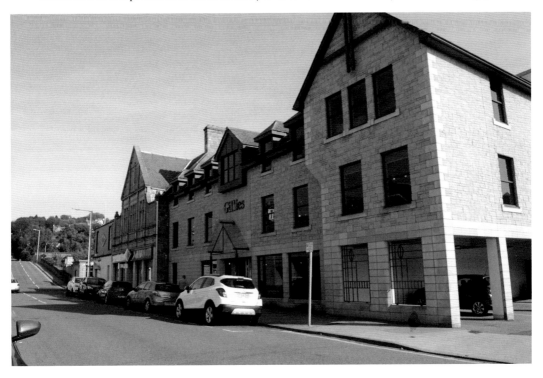

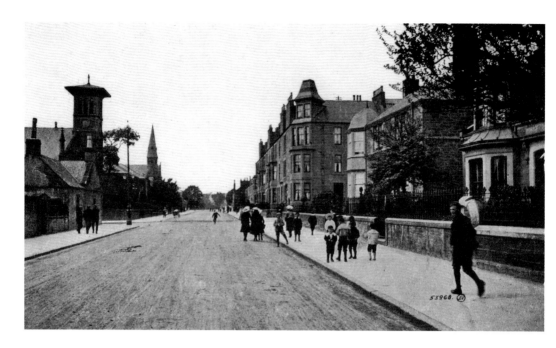

West Brook Street

Despite expansion over the years, Broughty Ferry manages to retain a village feel. Brook Street may be a busy shopping street but travel a short distance in either direction and you will find yourself in a quiet residential area. This scene at the west end is largely unchanged, although the West Church with its square tower in the earlier picture has been demolished. In 1962, its congregation united with that of St Stephen's, whose traditional spire is visible in both photographs.

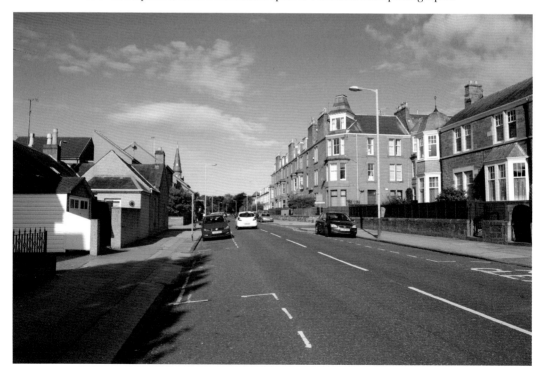

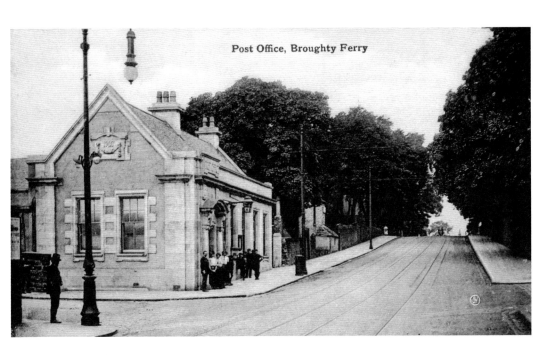

Post Office, Broughty Ferry

The Post Office, Queen Street

The date on the outside of the post office building in Queen Street is given as 1907 and this view dates from soon after that time. By the time of the modern photograph, the building has gained an extra storey and has been extended but has lost its original function and become a bar and restaurant. Its past is commemorated, though, in the name of The Post Office Bar.

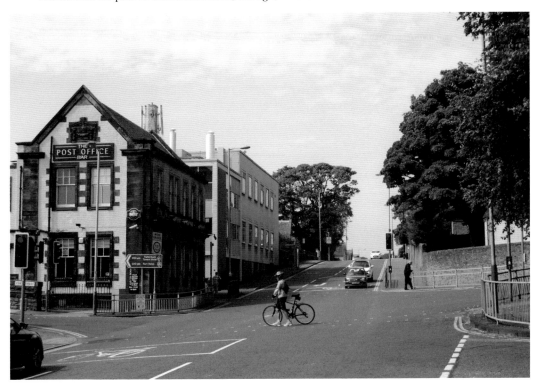

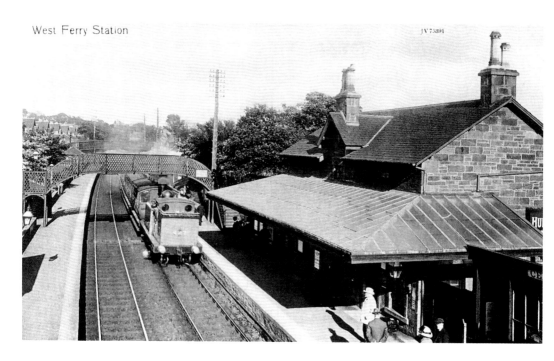

West Ferry Station

There was a railway station situated at West Ferry on the Dundee–Arbroath line for just over a century from the 1850s to the 1960s. Unlike many other defunct stations, including the one at Barnhill, the track and the station building remain today, making it easy to pinpoint the location.

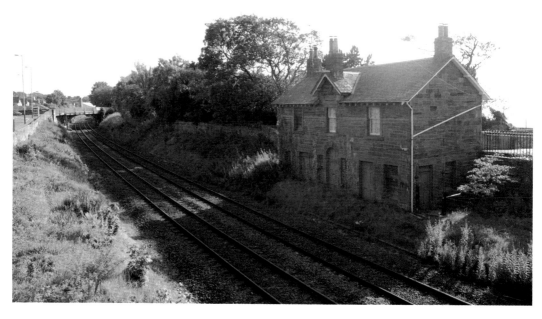

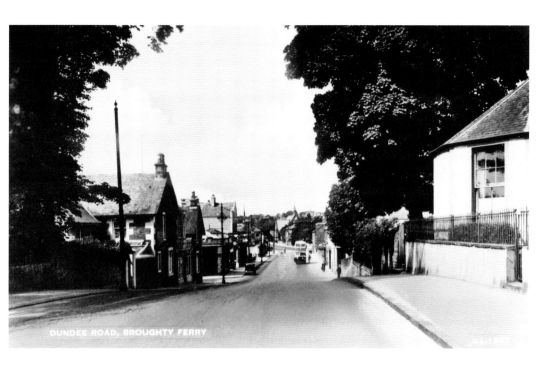

Dundee Road

The view from Queen Street looking westwards toward the Dundee road has changed little over the years. The house on the right-hand side, Brae Cottage, is now a residential home but was once home to Douglas Valentine, a member of the publishing company Valentine & Sons whose postcards were 'famous throughout the world' and who are responsible for many of the old views of Broughty Ferry that are preserved today.

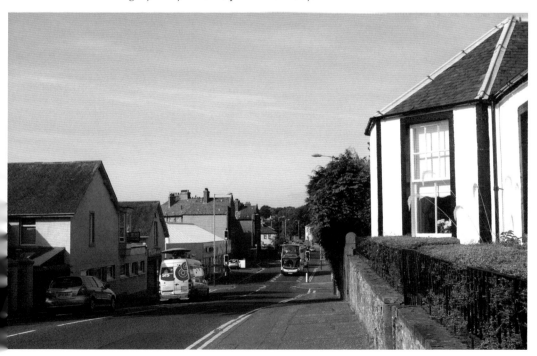

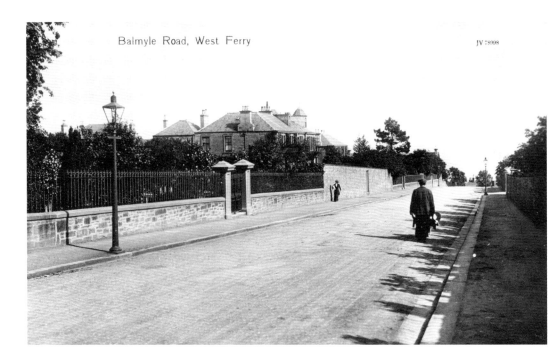

Balmyle Road

In the late nineteenth century Broughty Ferry attracted many wealthy residents, leading to its expansion to the east and west. Balmyle Road is typical of the residential streets of West Ferry – a suburb that remains just as desirable an area in which to live today as it did a century and more ago.

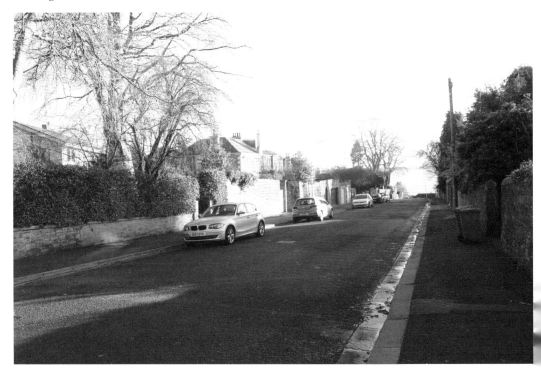

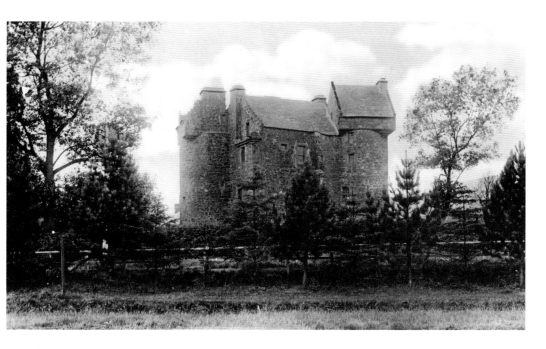

Claypotts Castle

John Strachan of Claypotts built Claypotts Castle between 1569 and 1588. When Strachan died in 1593, the estate was purchased by William Graham of Ballunie. It later came into the possession of the Grahams of Claverhouse, whose most famous member was John Graham, Viscount Dundee ('Bonnie Dundee' or 'Bloody Clavers'). After Claverhouse's death at the Battle of Killiecrankie in 1689, the forfeited castle was given to the Douglas family. It is now in the care of Historic Scotland.

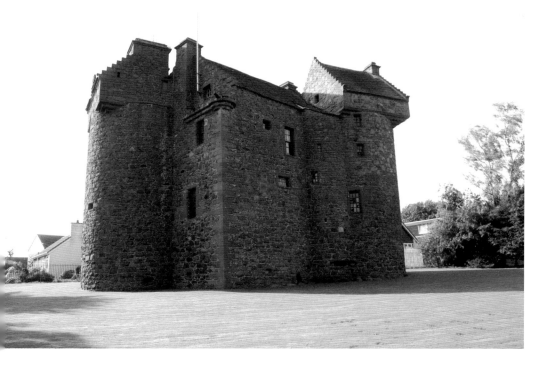

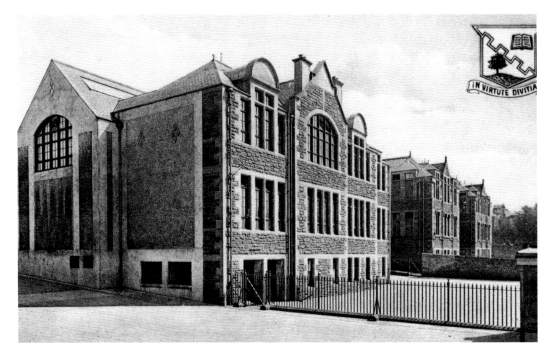

Grove Academy

Founded in the 1880s as a private school named Mr Swan's Grove Seminary, Grove Academy came under the authority of the local School Board in 1889 and has long enjoyed an excellent reputation. The old buildings depicted on this postcard remain standing today as part of a larger campus that includes the Eastern Primary School, but the modern photograph features the new Grove Academy which was opened in 2010.

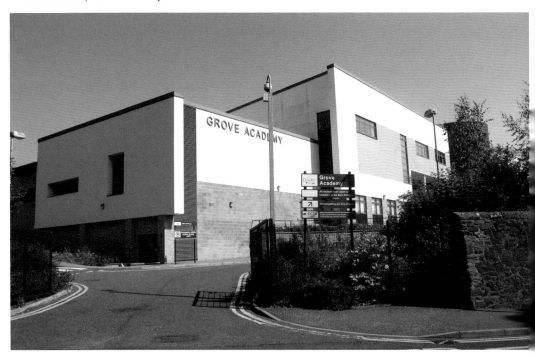

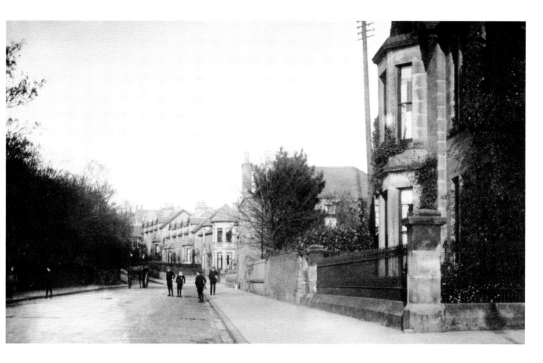

Seafield Road

Seen here from its junction with Camperdown Street, Seafield Road has given its name to a popular residential district. On the left-hand side of the old photograph are the grounds of a mansion called Seafield House. This site is now occupied by the new Grove Academy buildings.

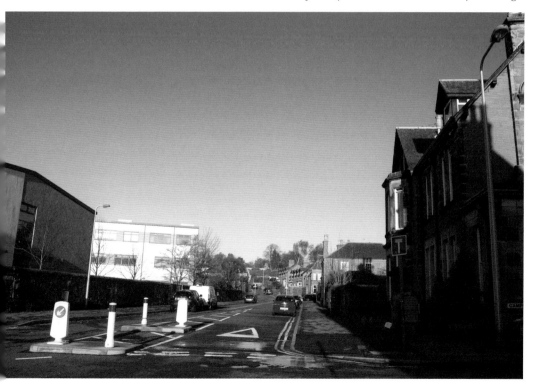

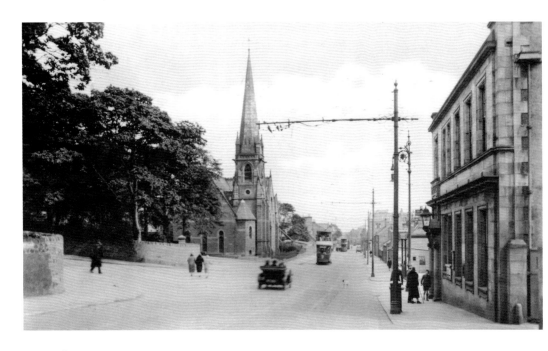

Queen Street

This 1920s view looking east along Queen Street has not changed much in its outward appearance except for the nature and volume of the traffic on the road. However, just as the post office building is no longer used for its original function, the Queen Street United Free Church buildings on the left-hand side of the picture have been home to an Indian restaurant since 1979.

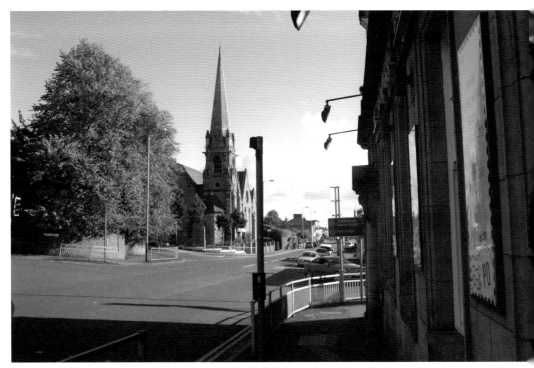

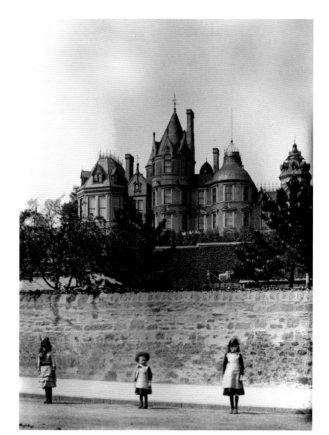

Carbet Castle

In 1861 Joseph Grimond of
Bowbridge Works bought Kerbat
House and extended it to the east
and west in French renaissance
style to produce Carbet Castle,
one of Broughty Ferry's famous
'jute palaces'. Falling victim to dry
rot, it was gradually demolished
until only the west wing was left
standing. This final section was
demolished in 1984. Luxury flats
have now been built on the site in
a style that echoes the Grimond
mansion.

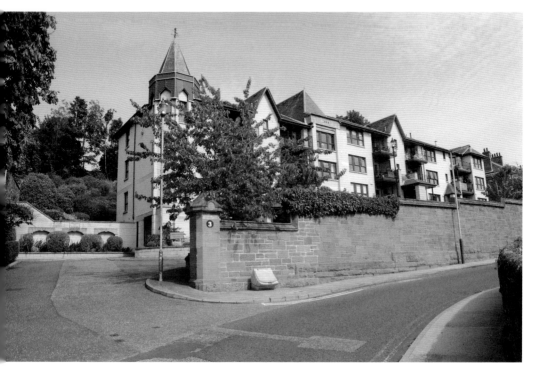

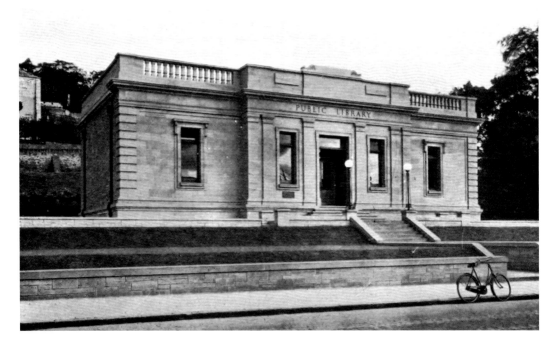

Broughty Ferry Library

In 1923, the local council bought some ground from the then proprietor of Carbet Castle at the cost of £600 for the purpose of building a library. Broughty Ferry branch library was opened in 1928 and was designed by James McLellan Brown, Dundee's depute city architect. Though it appears the same outwardly, the building has been adapted and expanded over the years and an extension to the rear can be seen in the recent photograph.

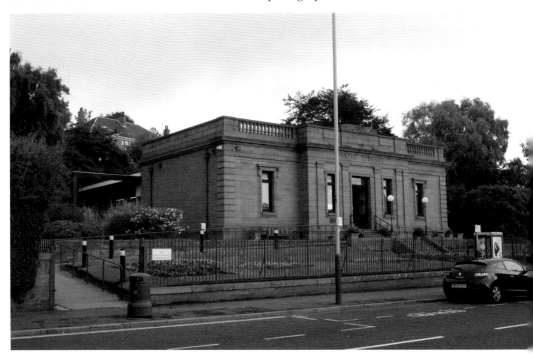

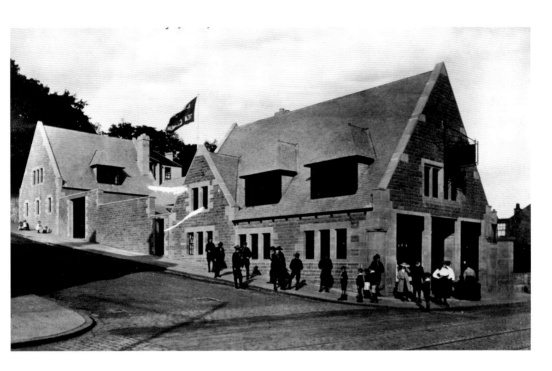

Loftus Tea Rooms

David Wallace was a baker, particularly famous in Dundee for his pies. In 1910, Wallace bought Loftus House in Gray Street and later opened the Loftus Tea Rooms in the grounds at the junction with Queen Street. The Tea Rooms had a hall on the first floor, which for many years was a popular venue for all sorts of functions and parties. A block of flats now occupies the site.

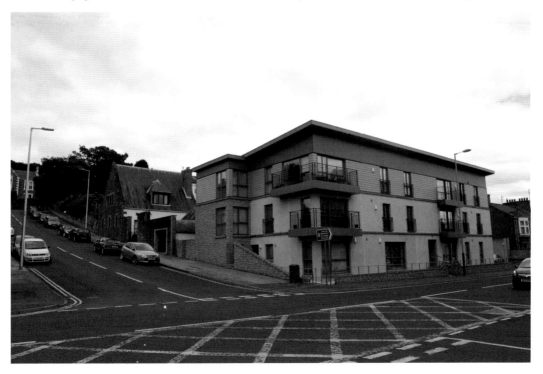

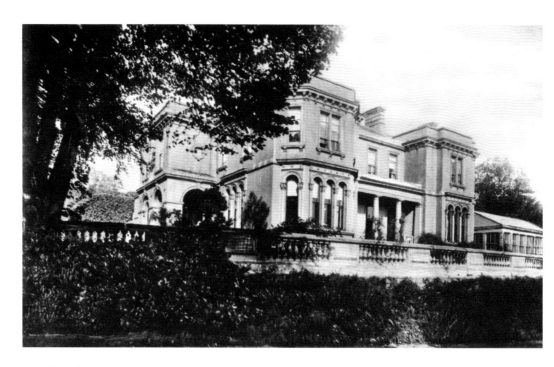

Dunalastair

At one time a Gilroy family mansion, Dunalastair in Hill Street was purchased by the Black Watch in 1920 and used as a holiday home for soldiers' families. In 1984, following a decrease in the popularity of traditional seaside holidays, the property was sold and converted into flats.

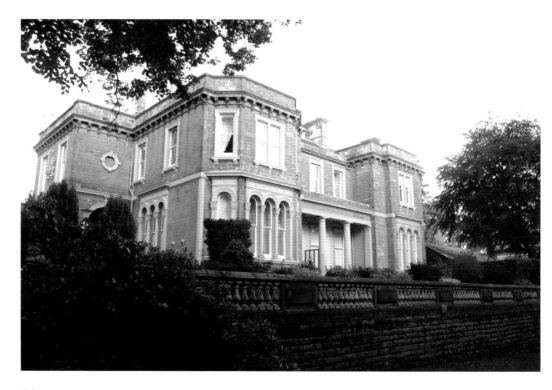

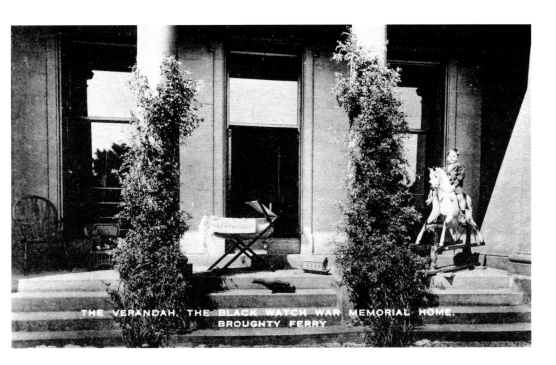

THE VERANDAH, THE BLACK WATCH WAR MEMORIAL HOME,
BROUGHTY FERRY

Dunalastair

The former connection to the Black Watch is evident from the regiment's badge which still adorns the building. It is likely that the small boy on the rocking horse in the older view had, in common with most of the children who holidayed here in the early days, lost his father in the First World War.

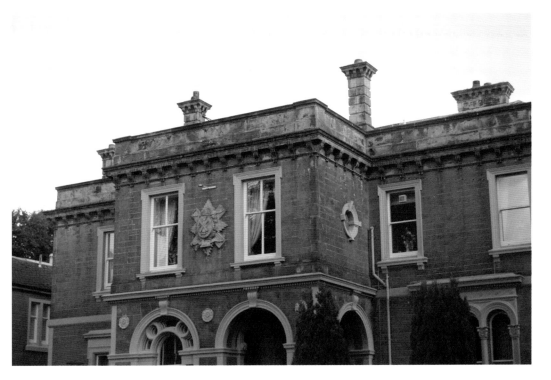

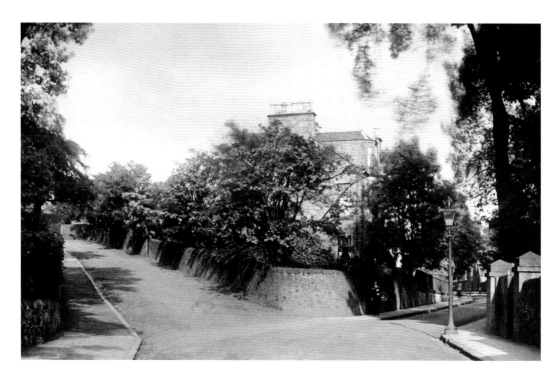

Dick Street/ Camphill Road

The junction of Dick Street and Camphill Road has changed little over the years. The disappearance of many of the trees though gives the scene a less rural feel, and the grit container is testament to the difficulties encountered by motor transport in bad weather, something that those who first chose to build their houses in this hilly terrain could not have foreseen.

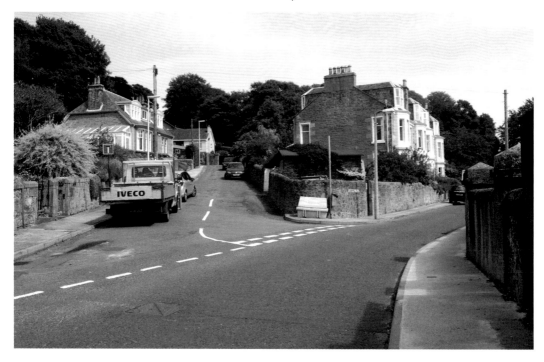

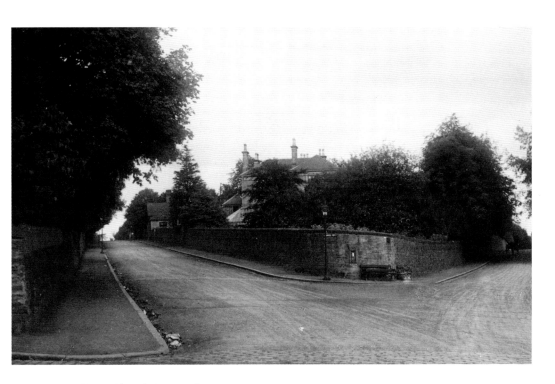

Camphill Road/Bughties Road

A little further along Camphill Road and we reach another fork in the road, this time the junction is with Bughties Road. The wall in the recent photograph still bears the signs of having been rebuilt following an accident in 2013. It was feared at the time that the historic postbox might be permanently closed but local pressure ensured its survival.

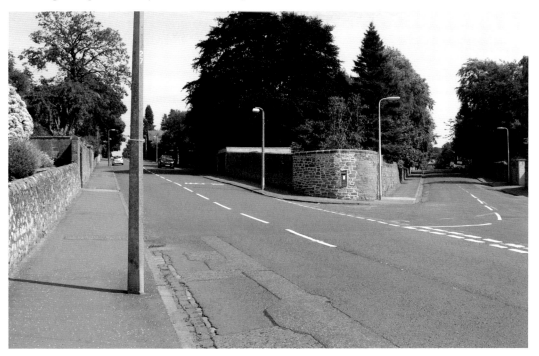

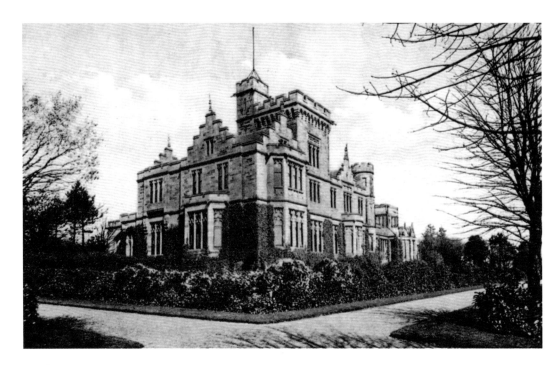

Castleroy

The largest and most flamboyant of the so-called jute places, Castleroy was built in 1867 for the Gilroy family who owned Tay Works. During the Second World War it was used to accommodate Polish forces. It came into the ownership of Dundee Corporation in 1946, but dry rot led to its demolition in the 1950s. The more modest properties of Castleroy Crescent are built on ground once owned by the Gilroys and along with Castleroy Road serve to commemorate the name.

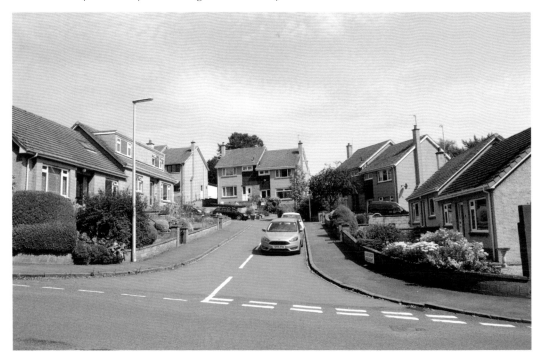

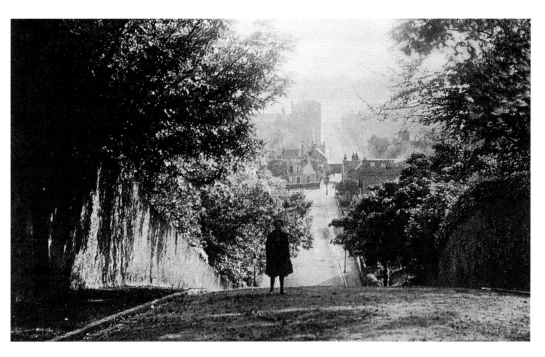

Whinny Brae

Although it begins at Monifieth Road, Whinny Brae does not truly begin to climb uphill until after the former Eastern Primary School, giving rise to its famously steep incline. Viewed here from Camphill Road, it is easy to see why this section of the road is no longer open to traffic.

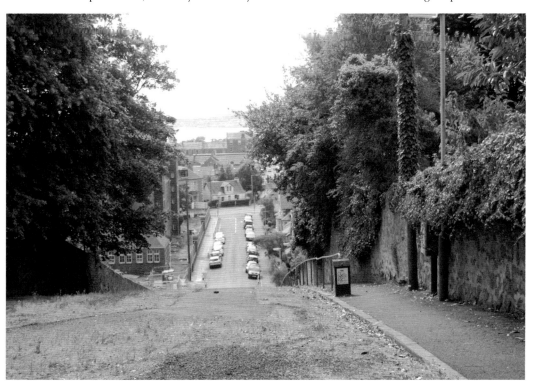

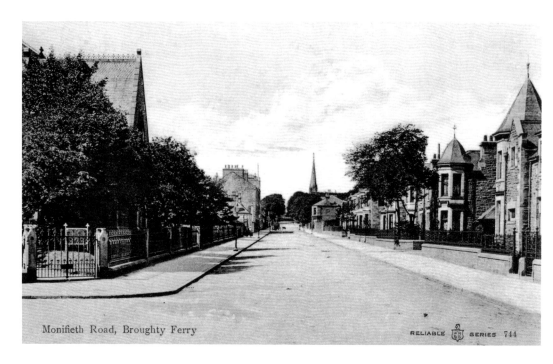

Monifieth Road, Broughty Ferry

RELIABLE SERIES 744

Queen Street from Monifieth Road

The church on the left of this view along Queen Street from its junction with Monifieth Road and St Vincent, known as the East Church, was opened in 1865 to house a Free Church congregation. In 1900 the union of the Free Church and the United Presbyterian Church produced the United Free Church. In 1929 the UF Church, in turn, reunited with the Church of Scotland. The congregations of the East Parish Church and St Aiden's were united in 2005 to form The New Kirk.

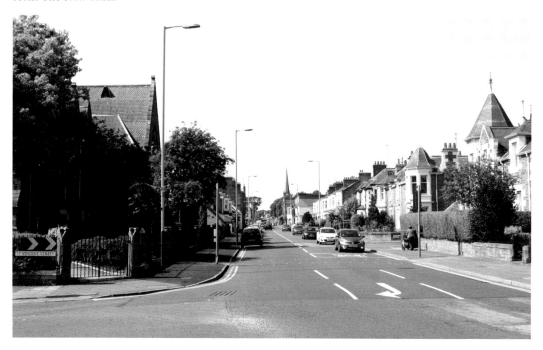

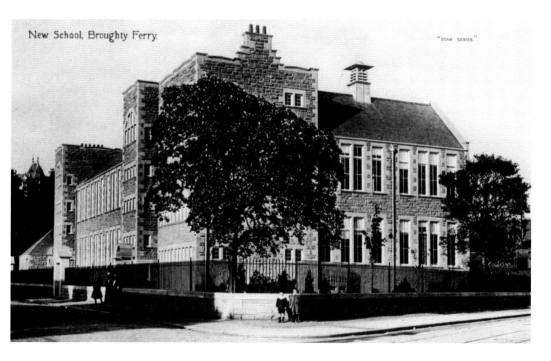

New School, Broughty Ferry.   "STAR SERIES."

Eastern Primary School, Whinny Brae

In 1911, the Eastern School moved to new premises, built to a design by the Dundee architect James Hendry Langlands. The caption on this old postcard refers to the 'new' school so it presumably dates from around that time. The school occupied this site for one hundred years, moving to Camperdown Street beside Grove Academy in 2011. The former site has since been converted into flats.

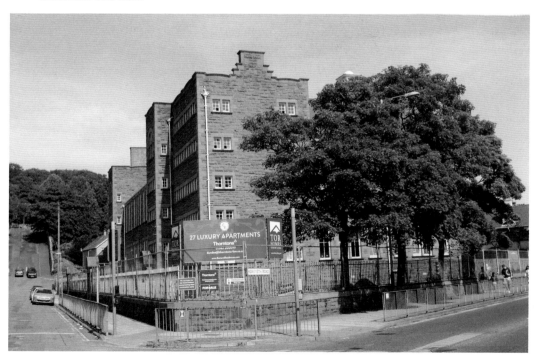

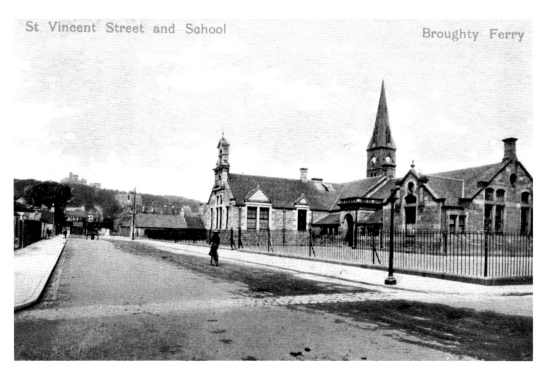

Eastern Primary School, St Vincent Street
The Eastern Public School was built in 1873 and occupied this site at St Vincent Street until increasing pupil numbers precipitated the move to new premises. The school building is now occupied by a firm of undertakers. When the lower photograph was taken in August 2015, flats were being built at the north end of the site, necessitating that the image be captured at a slightly different angle.

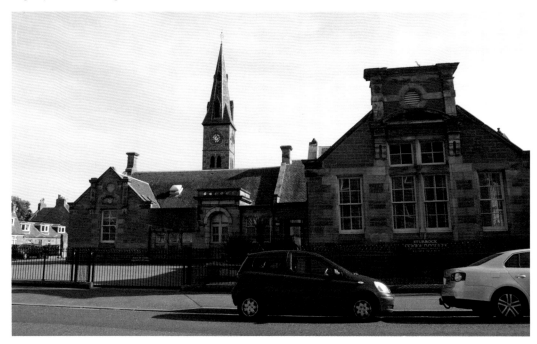

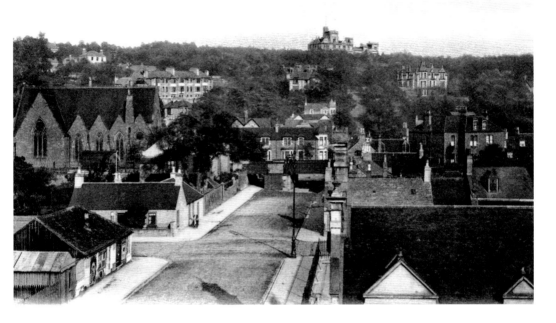

St Vincent Street

Castleroy is visible on top of the hill in this view of St Vincent Street from the early 1900s, but has since vanished from the skyline. The street was named to commemorate the British victory at the Battle of Cape St Vincent in 1797. The Portuguese cape itself was named after Saint Vincent of Saragossa – a third-century Christian martyr.

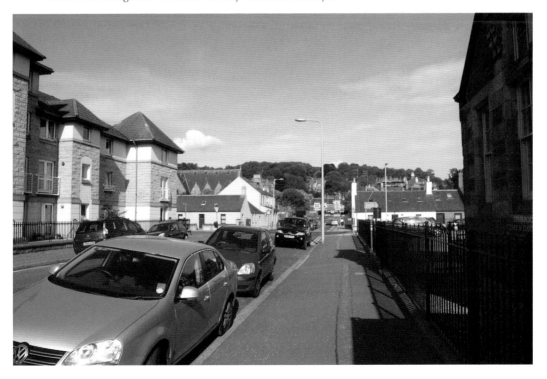

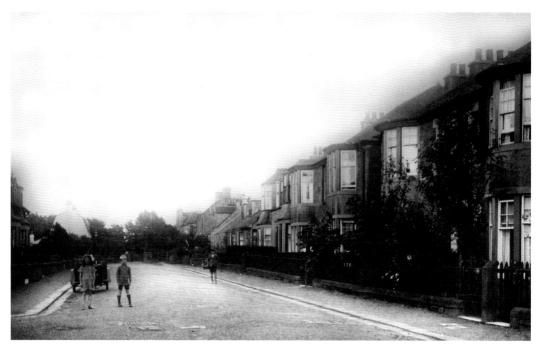

Ramsay Street (formerly Ramsay Park)

In the 1920s cars were few and far between, even in a relatively affluent suburb such as Broughty Ferry. A solitary vehicle can be glimpsed behind the little girl in this view. By the early twenty-first century, however, even a quiet side street such as Ramsay Street is dominated by the motorcar.

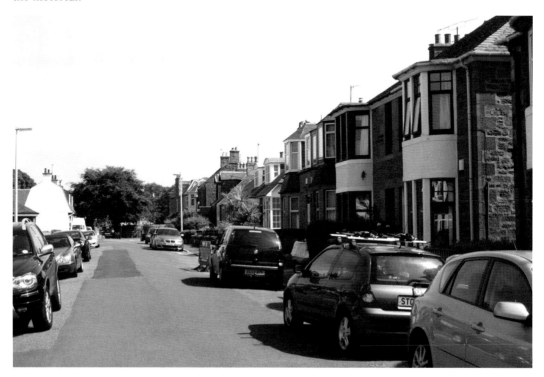

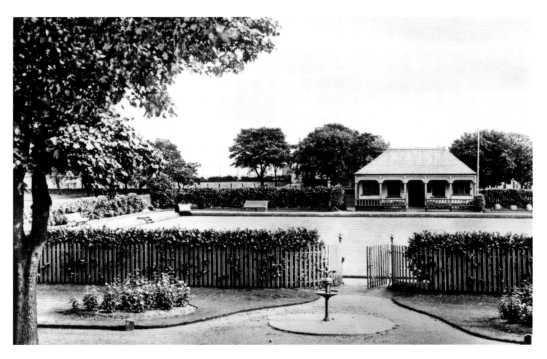

Orchar Park

This 6 ½-acre recreation ground was acquired for the town a few years after the site at Reres Hill on the other side of Monifieth Road. This public space benefited from the generosity of Broughty Ferry's chief magistrate James Guthrie Orchar, who gifted the walls and railings for the park which now bears his name.

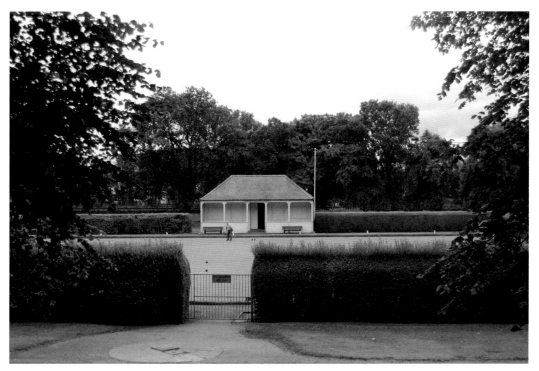

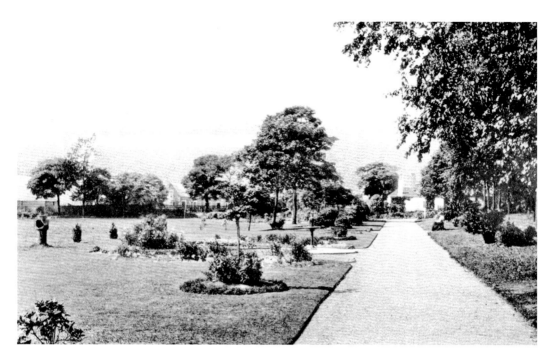

Orchar Park

The view of the northernmost section of the park today shows a layout that closely reflects that of the early years of the twentieth century. The one major change is the enclosure of the bowling green which was opened on 13 May 1911 by Provost Lindsay. The cost to the local council of the green (bowl house, furnishings etc) was £657 6s 11d.

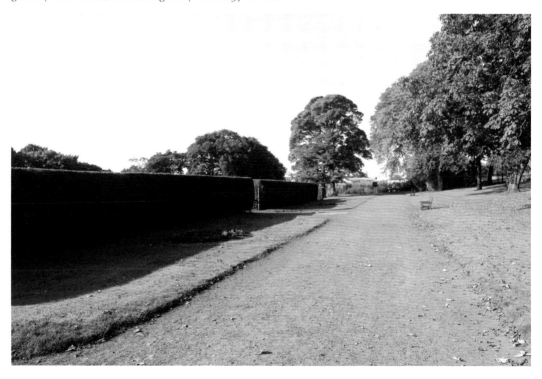

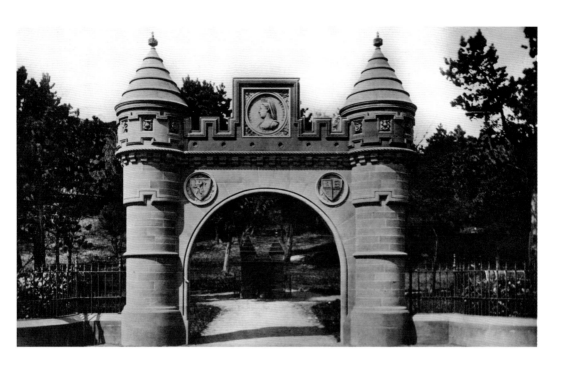

Jubilee Arch

The archway that marks the entrance to Reres Hill Park was presented by James Guthrie Orchar in 1887 to mark the Golden Jubilee of Queen Victoria's accession to the throne. It was designed by Orchar's friend, the architect T. S. Robertson. The long-defunct drinking fountain, which can be seen through the arch and reflects its style, was presented at the same time

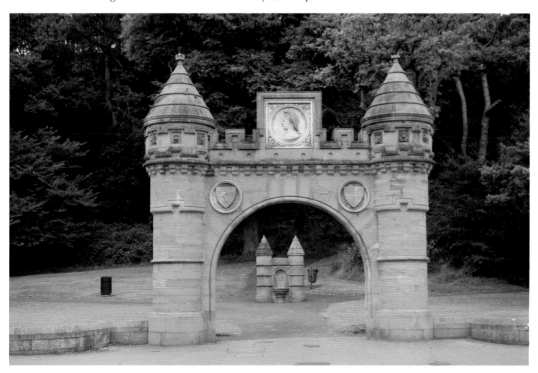

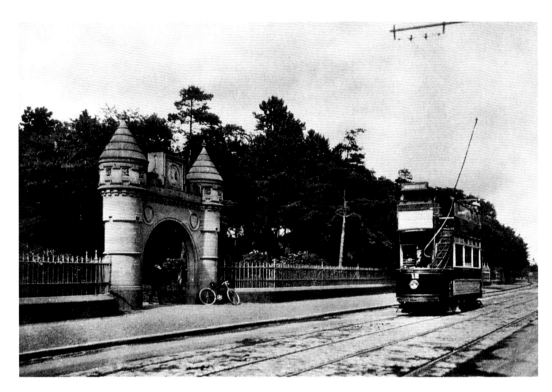

Jubilee Arch, Monifieth Road

The Jubilee Arch is shown in its wider context in this early twentieth-century view. The railings on either side, in common with park railings throught the country, would have been removed during the Second World War. The tramcar in the older image is heading towards Monifieth from Dundee – a route which began in 1905 – while in the recent photograph the bus is going in the opposite direction.

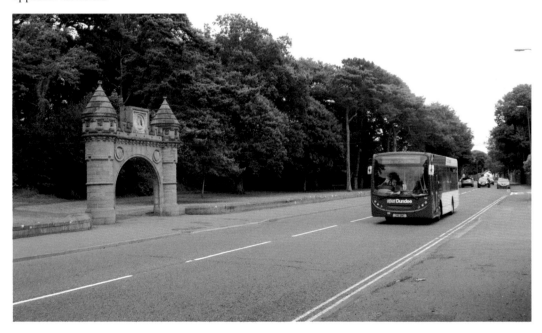

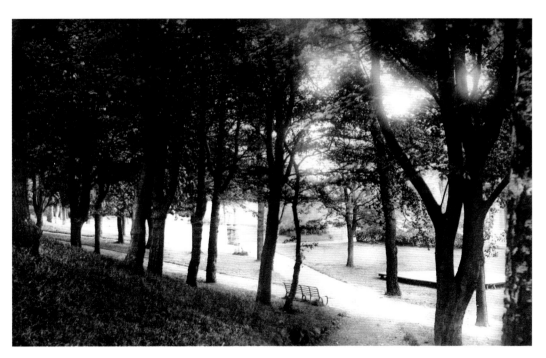

Reres Hill Park
Previously the property of the Earl of Dalhousie, this 6 ½-acre site became a public park in 1868. The hill itself, which was once immortalised in the words of an old folk ballad 'The Back o' Reres Hill', remains a popular place of recreation today.

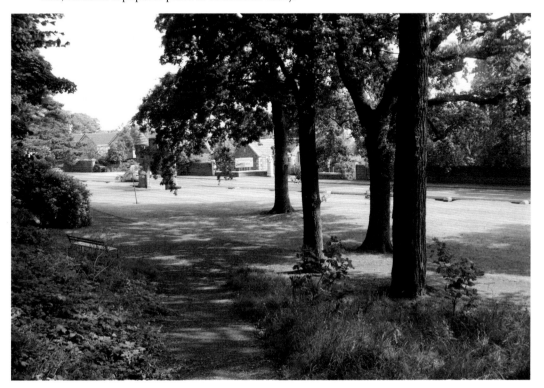

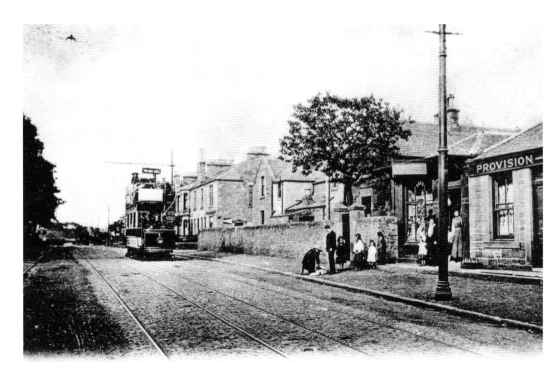

Dalhousie Road Barnhill Looking East

This view looking eastward along Dalhousie Road shows Barnhill's original post office, which was situated just beyond the railway bridge. Like the bridge itself, no trace remains of the post office building. Barnhill retains a post office however, situated at the Campfield Square shops at Nursery Road.

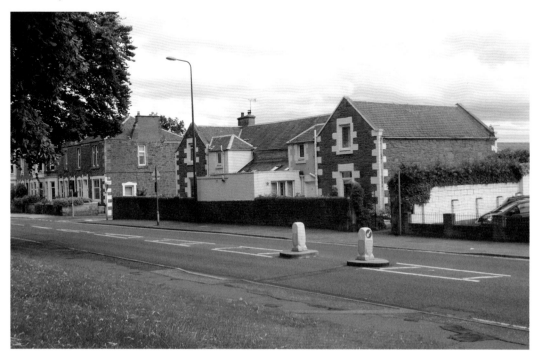

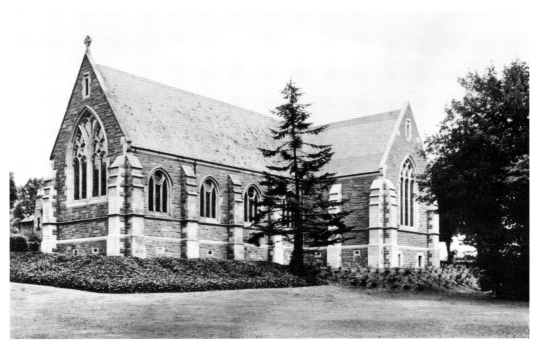

St Margaret's Church, Barnhill

Originally a chapel of ease serving the western section of the parish of Monifieth, St Margaret's was founded in 1884. The original congregation worshipped in a building made of corrugated iron and known as the Tin Kirk. St Margaret's became a parish in its own right in March 1907.

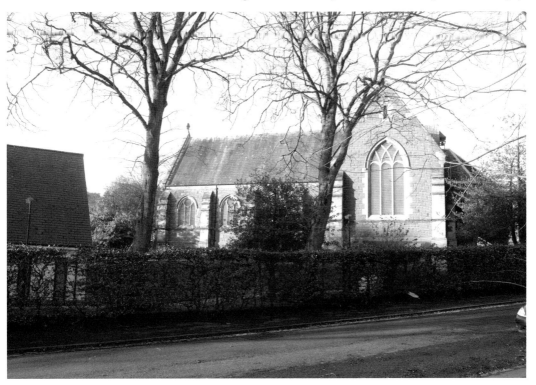

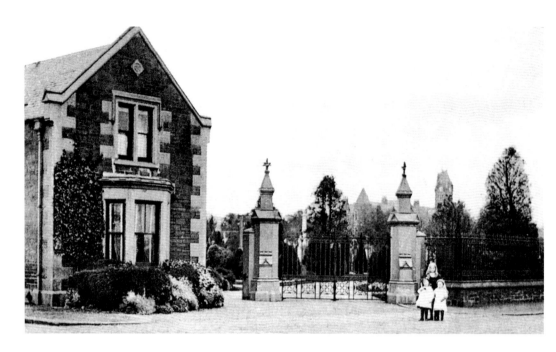

Barnhill Cemetery

Following the closure of the old burial ground at Fisher Street, Barnhill Cemetery was opened in 1869. Unlike those belonging to some of Dundee's other parks and cemeteries, the lodge house remains intact. Just visible past the right-hand-side gatepost in the older picture is the Convalescent Home which was built in then rural Barnhill with funds provided by jute baron Sir David Baxter. Following the demolition of the home, housing was built on the site.

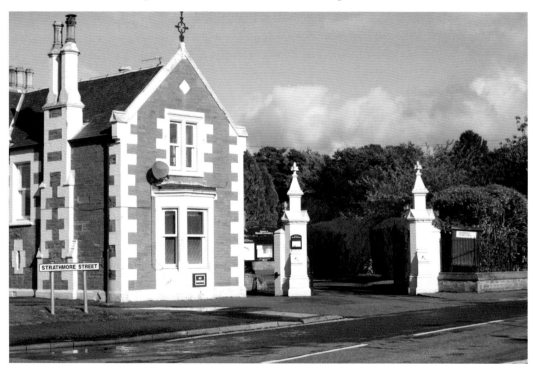

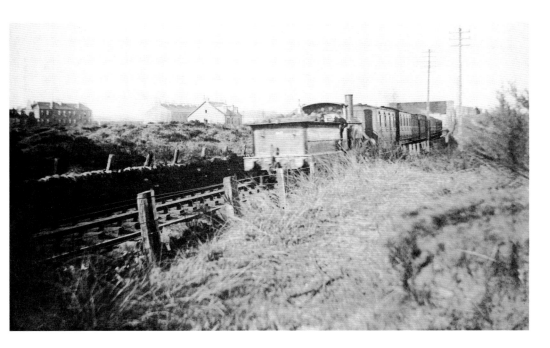

Barnhill from the Links

This rare archive photograph of Barnhill dates from a time when the area was mainly open countryside. Only a single house and a terraced block in what is now Collingwood Street are visible between the railway line and Dalhousie Road. The built-up nature of the area prevents a photograph being taken from the same angle, so the lower picture is of the Barnhill Rock Garden which now occupies the land to the south of the railway line.

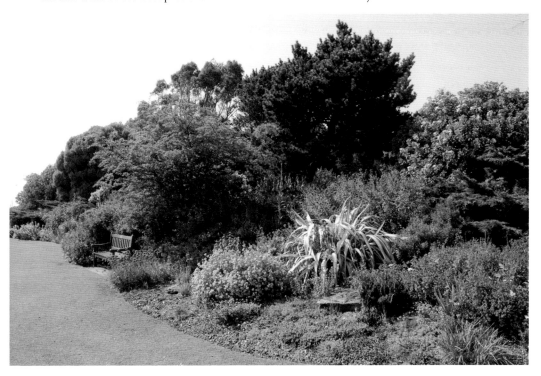

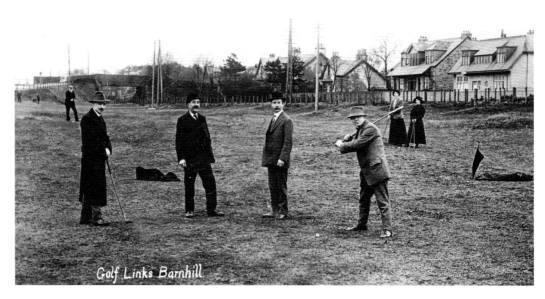

Golf Links Barnhill

Barnhill Golf Course

A nine-hole golf course once occupied a stretch of ground running alongside the Dundee–Aberdeen railway line at Barnhill. This side of the course has changed less in appearance than its western counterpart, though a children's play park occupies the area just behind the camera's position.

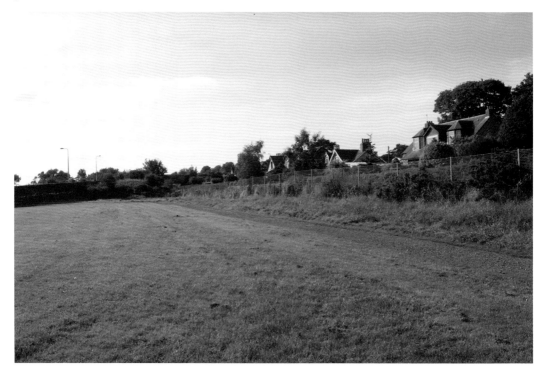

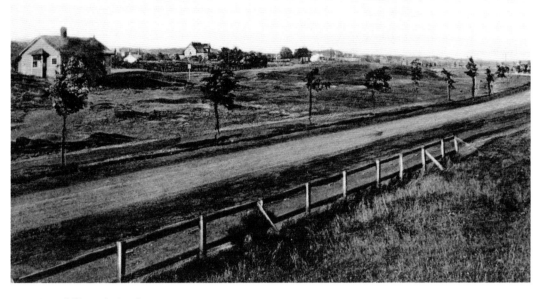

Barnhill Rock Garden

While five of the old golf course's holes were situated to the east of Bridge Street, the other four were to the west. In 1955, work began to convert the western part of the course into a rock garden, which continues to flourish today. The last remnant of the golf course to survive was the old clubhouse, which was destroyed by a fire in 1993.

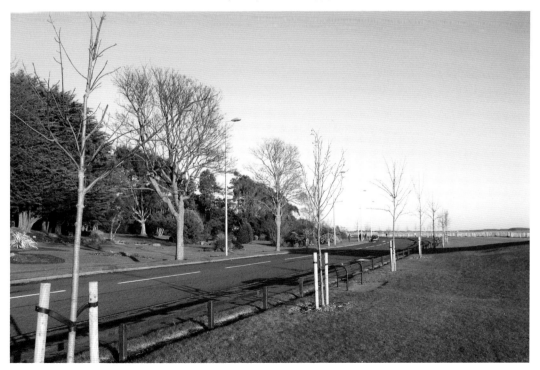

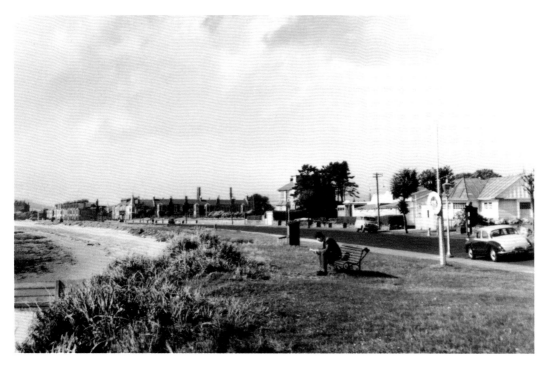

The Chalet

In the background of the archive photograph can be seen what was originally the Chalet Refreshment Rooms and later the Chalet Ballroom. It was later replaced by the building that housed the Sands Discotheque and Buddies Nightclub. This site is now occupied by luxury flats.

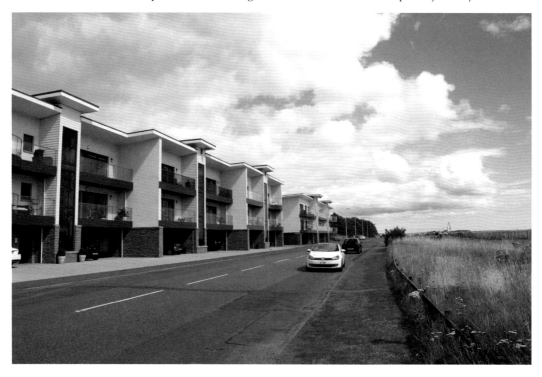

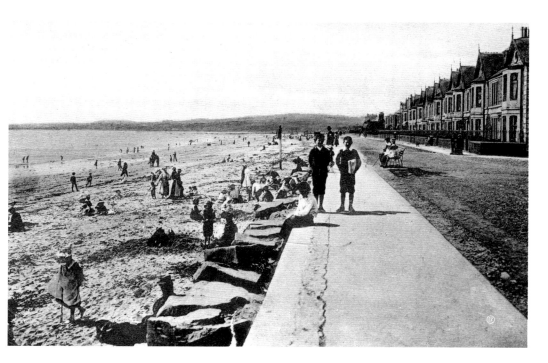

The Esplanade

Broughty Ferry's esplanade was completed in 1894. Such esplanades or promenades were popular in the late Victorian and Edwardian periods, allowing people to enjoy a walk along the seafront whether the tide was in or out and without the need to even venture on to the sand. It is still a pleasant walk today, though the grassy dunes mean that the beach has disappeared from view at this point.

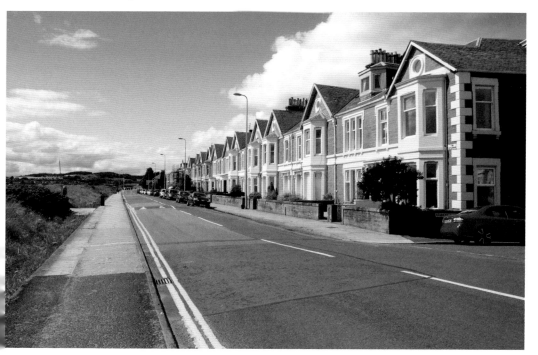

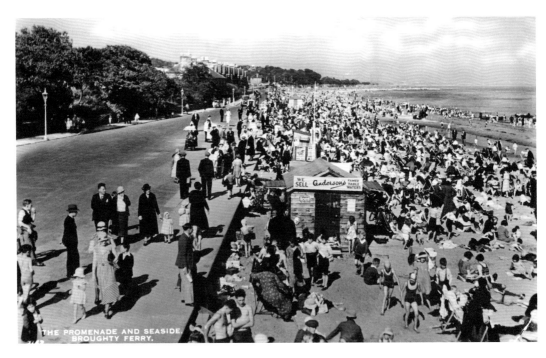

The Sands Looking East

In the latter part of the nineteenth century, Broughty Ferry began to attract tourists from all over Scotland as well as day-trippers from Dundee. Its beaches remain popular today, though thankfully, a little less crowded than in the past.

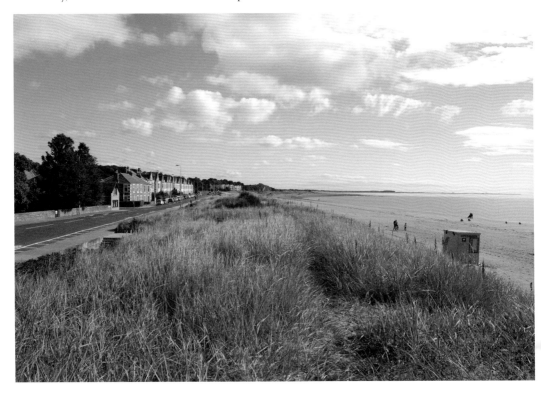

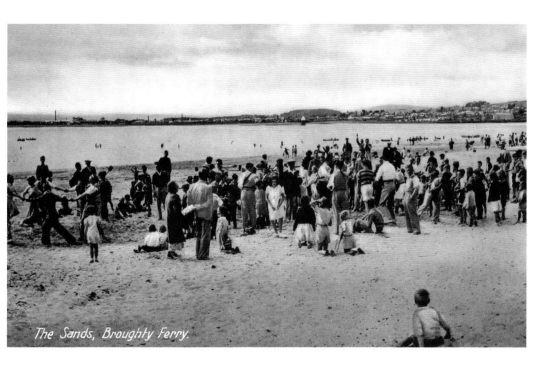

The Sands, Broughty Ferry.

The Sands Looking West

The lower photograph looking from Broughty Ferry sands across the river to Tayport was taken on a sunny August morning in 2014, but does not feature even a single person walking by. The older picture, which dates from around the 1930s, shows how difficult it would have been to capture such a clear view for much of the twentieth century.

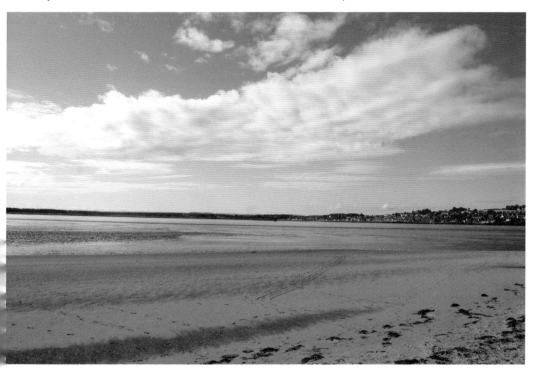

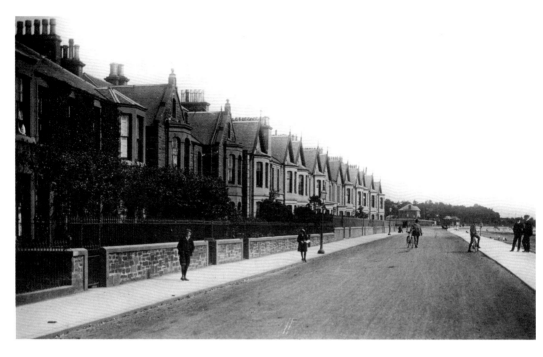

Newington Terrace

Not only were houses on the Esplanade numbered, the individual terraced blocks were given their own names and numbers, thus making No. 1 Newington Terrace (the first of the houses with a round window between the eaves) also No. 7 Esplanade.

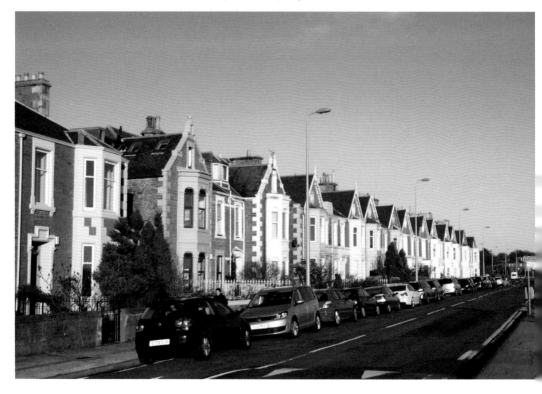

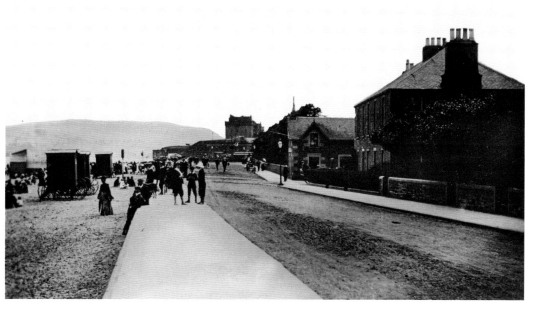

Esplanade

Visible on the beach in the archive view here are several bathing machines. These consisted of a small shed-like structure on wheels and date from a time when women bathed in specially designated areas to protect their modesty. The bathing machine had a door behind and another in front and provided space for the user to change in privacy. The machine would then be wheeled into the water where the bather could emerge away from prying eyes.

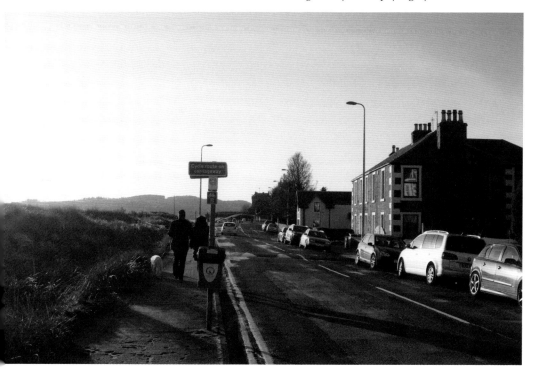

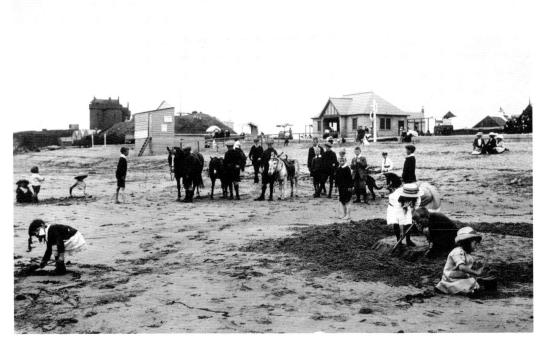

Beach

Donkey rides were a popular feature of seaside resorts from Victorian times but today are a thing of the past at Broughty Ferry. Indeed, access to the award-winning beach is restricted even for dogs. One thing that does survive though is the old beach shelter, now a public convenience.

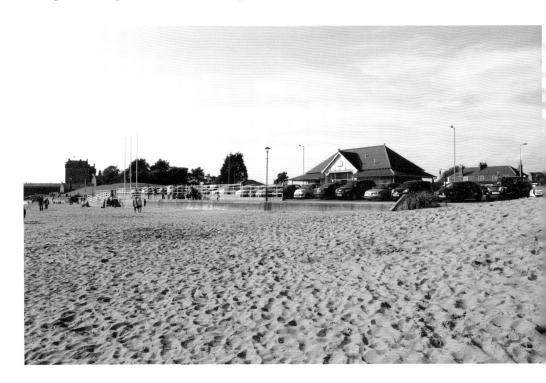

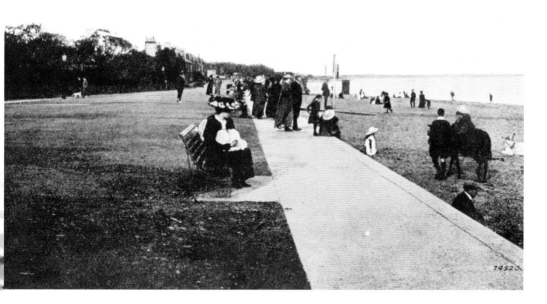

Esplanade

A final glance along the beach and Esplanade from a time when the seaside holiday was arguably at its most popular. Whatever changes there have been over the years in Broughty Ferry, many of the features that attracted our ancestors to spend their spare time there, such as the beach itself, remain intact. It is to be hoped that this book will have encouraged people to take another look at what was once styled 'The Brighton of the North'.

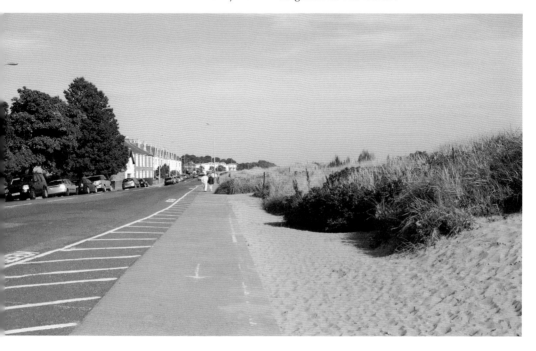

Acknowledgements

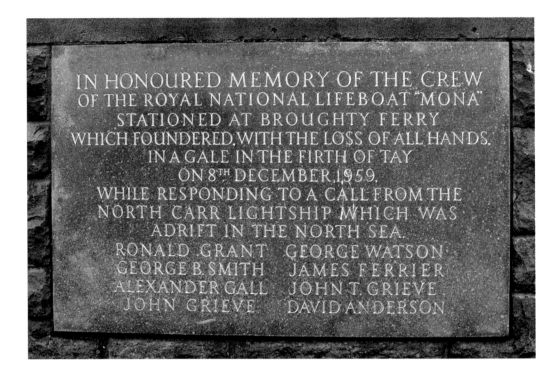

IN HONOURED MEMORY OF THE CREW
OF THE ROYAL NATIONAL LIFEBOAT "MONA"
STATIONED AT BROUGHTY FERRY
WHICH FOUNDERED, WITH THE LOSS OF ALL HANDS,
IN A GALE IN THE FIRTH OF TAY
ON 8TH DECEMBER 1959,
WHILE RESPONDING TO A CALL FROM THE
NORTH CARR LIGHTSHIP WHICH WAS
ADRIFT IN THE NORTH SEA.
RONALD GRANT   GEORGE WATSON
GEORGE B. SMITH   JAMES FERRIER
ALEXANDER GALL   JOHN T. GRIEVE
JOHN GRIEVE   DAVID ANDERSON

The archive images are from my own collection, except for those on the following pages : 18, 19, 21, 27, 28, 32, 33, 35, 37, 48, 49, 51 and 53 – Dundee City Archives

Many thanks to Iain Flett, Martin Allan, Alex Banks and John Gray for their assistance with these.

Pages 9, 23 and 63 – Libraries, Leisure and Culture Dundee (from the Alexander Wilson Collection). Thanks to Maureen Hood for her help.

All of the modern photographs were taken by me except for the one on page 13 which is courtesy of Ye Amphibious Ancients Bathing Association. Many thanks to Joyce McIntosh for her assistance with this.

My apologies for any inadvertent omission in attribution.